Prais

THE PRINCIPLED PRINCIPAL

"In my work with schools, I have learned that the principal of a school is the key to the culture and consequently the outcomes of the school. In *The Principled Principal*, Zoul and McConnell illustrate the beliefs and behaviors that are practiced by the best schools and principals. All great school leaders know that success begins by looking inward. Well researched and full of engaging stories and practical examples, this book is a must-read for every school leader."

—Sean Covey, international best-selling author of *The 7 Habits of Highly Effective Teens* and *The Leader in Me*

"If I were asked to identify a set of core values principals must possess to successfully lead their schools, I would point to *The Principled Principal*. Jeff Zoul and Anthony McConnell have clearly articulated the critical attributes and behaviors school leaders must demonstrate to lead with integrity, compassion, and purpose. This book will speak to principals wherever they are in their career. Aspiring school leaders will receive a picture of what's to come. New school leaders will have a resource to guide them. Veterans will be encouraged and validated."

—Jason Leahy, executive director, Illinois Principals' Association

"In *The Principled Principal*, Jeffrey Zoul and Anthony McConnell lay out ten principles that every school principal needs. Based on their many years of experience in leadership, Zoul and McConnell provide practical steps that readers can put into practice immediately. This book is for practitioners written by practitioners."

—Peter DeWitt, Ed.D., author, consultant, presenter

"The key to improving our education system begins with leadership. A great principal will create a great school. In *The Principled Principal*, Jeffrey Zoul and Anthony McConnell provide school leaders the road map for improvement, transformation, and success. This book is a must-read for anyone wanting to positively impact their school."

—Jon Gordon, best-selling author of *The Energy Bus* and *The Power of Positive Leadership*

"What type of principal leadership actions influence learning for all in our learning communities? This is the question that Jeff Zoul and Anthony McConnell help us explore and understand in *The Principled Principal*. Jeff and Anthony guide the reader through the most impactful core leadership principles to which successful principals adhere as they work with their teams to create the best conditions for teaching and learning. These core values range from communication and harmony, to management and the importance of self leadership.

"This book is a guide for all who seek to lead with impact— aspiring, new, and experienced school leaders. As an experienced principal, I was able to relate and learn from the many great school principals featured in *The Principled Principal*. I'm confident that you will, too."

—Rosa Isiah, Ed. D., principal, Smith Elementary School (CA)

"The research on the impact of school leadership is clear. Dynamic, collaborative leadership is foundational in creating schools that are future ready and those that provide the learning experiences today's modern learners need to thrive in tomorrow's world. In *The Principled Principal*, Zoul and McConnell lay out ten principles for leading exceptional schools, offering insight gained as long-time practitioners while infusing powerful stories from nationally recognized leaders and the resources needed to support your school's future success. Transforming teaching and learning at your school starts with you, and this book will guide you each step of the way."

—Thomas C. Murray, director of innovation, Future Ready Schools, and coauthor of *Learning Transformed*

"*The Principled Principal* is such a powerful and meaningful way to frame this critical leadership position within the educational landscape. All effective leaders must be principled and intentional about all that they do so they can best serve their community. The book stresses the importance of an effective leader primarily being an engaged and active learner. The notion of a leader as a work in progress really stood out because it speaks to the importance that a leader is not 'fixed' or 'finished' but instead is always learning, growing, and improving. This text also successfully addresses how school leaders can affect change—from meaningful hiring practices to intentional communication practices. The overarching theme of this book speaks to the importance of culture and how culture influences what people believe, how they feel, and how they act. Culture is the key to effective leadership!

"Overall, this book is a practical step-by-step guide for new educational leaders and a powerful resource for those who have been leading for years, thanks to the innovative approaches offered throughout. I especially loved the 3-2-1 activity at the end of each chapter where practitioners offer their experiences to support the theoretical underpinnings of the book. I highly recommend it!"

—Tony Sinanis, educator, author, and speaker

"*The Principled Principal* is the perfect companion for school leaders who are hoping to move practice from out behind a desk and into the heart of their schools. It reminds us that education is a profession about people—our students, our colleagues, our communities. As such, being a principal is not only about leading people but also helping them grow—and helping yourself grow along the way."

—Jennie Magiera, author of *Courageous Edventures*

"Zoul and McConnell provide both current and aspiring school leaders indispensable guidance for success in *The Principled Principal*. Their ten Principal Principles offer the framework upon which educational leaders build rapidly improving schools. The expertise gathered from practitioners in the field, and shared via stories and anecdotes, offers a behind-the-scenes look at the master principal's playbook. A must-read!"

—Weston Kieschnick, author of *Bold School* and senior fellow, International Center for Leadership in Education

"This is a book that every principal (or those who desire to be) should keep on his/her desk. It is practical, powerful, and driven by common sense thinkers who have done the job and know the work. The writers hit a home run in the first line of the book, 'schools exist primarily for the students they serve' and continue rounding the bases in future chapters."

—Jason L. Branch, Ph.D., superintendent, Oconee County (GA) Schools

"As a person who lives and leads by principles, many of which were highlighted in this book, *The Principled Principal* resonated with me on so many levels. It is evident that the knowledge shared throughout the book is gleaned from several years of personal experience. The 3-2-1 resources at the end of each chapter nicely tie together the principles discussed. This book will appeal to leaders regardless of their experience level or setting. It will surely serve as a guide for personal reflection and growth for new and veteran principals alike."

—Sanée Bell, Ed.D., principal, Houston, Texas

"Filled with personal and professional anecdotes, a genuine sense of guidance, support, and mentoring, this is the perfect read for a department/school leadership team, the model textbook for a supervisory/administrative leadership course, and the ideal gift for the future principal/school leader. In an era dedicated to continuous improvement, *The Principled Principal* guides principals toward five critical S's: student, staff, school, system, and one's own self-development."

—Guy Schumacher, superintendent, Libertyville (IL) School District 70

"*The Principled Principal* is an inspiring, impactful, and necessary read for any current or aspiring educational leader. Zoul and McConnell illustrate the importance of grasping sound principles as educational leaders to positively impact the entire school experience. The book provides practical resources and examples from phenomenal school leaders who demonstrate how the principles are critical to ongoing success and growth. Educational leadership is a challenging, yet noble profession. This book highlights the importance of staying true to the principles that best serve our students."

—Becky Ince, principal, Central Intermediate School and district curriculum director

"Jeff and Anthony have pulled off a difficult feat with their new book, *The Principled Principal*. Never once did I feel like I was turning pages. Rather, reading this book felt like a coffee shop chat among friends with an occasional guest dropping by from time to time, to add to the discussion. The authors' use of personal anecdotes, present-day analogies, and conversational language, was refreshing. Current and aspiring principals will have this book on their shelves for years to come."

—Jon Harper, assistant principal

"With *The Principled Principal*, Zoul and McConnell have crafted the perfect resource. Their principles serve as a guideline for launching rapid and sustainable change in our schools. Building upon the knowledge and expertise garnered from veterans in the field, the authors have provided the reader with a solid and reliable foundation for focused growth across the spectrum of academics, taking into account culture, data, and the importance of interpersonal connections. No instructional leader determined to see visible improvement in their school should be without this book. An exceptional read!"

—Stacy Hughes, assistant principal, Morgan County (AL) School District

THE
PRINCIPLED
PRINCIPAL

10 Principles for Leading Exceptional Schools

Jeffrey Zoul and Anthony McConnell

The Principled Principal

This book is available at special discounts when purchased in quantity for use as premiums, promotions, fundraisers, or for educational use. For inquiries and details, contact the publisher at books@daveburgessconsulting.com.

Published by Dave Burgess Consulting, Inc.
San Diego, CA
http://daveburgessconsulting.com

Cover Design by Genesis Kohler
Editing and Interior Design by My Writers' Connection

Library of Congress Control Number: 2017964466
Paperback ISBN: 978-1-946444-58-5
Ebook ISBN: 978-1-946444-59-2

DEDICATION

Jeff would like to dedicate this book to his daughter and favorite travel companion, Jordyn Campbell Zoul.

Anthony would like to dedicate this book to his wife, Cayce, and their two children, Aurelia and Anthony.

CONTENTS

Introduction

When you base your life on principles, most
of your decisions are already made before you
encounter them.

—Unknown

L ike most educators, we believe schools exist primarily for
the students they serve. In everything we do, we must
intentionally ask ourselves what is best for kids and how
the actions we take—or decide not to take—will impact our
students.

As principals, one of the most important actions we can
take to serve our students is to hire the very best teachers we
can find. Nothing impacts student success more than the quality of the teacher. Passionate teachers, skilled in both the art
and science of teaching, have the ability to dramatically impact
the lives of the children they serve. In fact, we tend to agree

with a statement we've often heard from Todd Whitaker, a well-known author and professor, that, ultimately, there are only two ways to improve the school: 1) Hire better teachers and 2) ensure the teachers currently in place continue to improve.

While we agree that teachers are indeed the most important variable impacting student success, we also maintain that the importance of school principals is a very close second. Although the impact of the principal may be more indirect than that of the classroom teacher, this impact is nearly as profound. Almost everything the school principal does—or does not do—has a direct impact on teachers who, in turn, more directly impact students. When strong principals are in place, they positively influence the school culture and the instructional quality of the teachers they lead; moreover, school leaders' impact on students contributes to 25 percent of the school's influence on a child's academic performance.

We have witnessed schools with almost identical demographic characteristics perform at distinctly different levels because of the leadership in place at those schools. We must do everything in our power to ensure that all schools in our nation are led by highly qualified and highly skilled professionals. We must further ensure that these men and women continue to grow professionally once they assume the principalship and receive the support they need.

The job of school principal in the twenty-first century is incredibly demanding and only becoming more challenging. The responsibilities of the principal are wide ranging and can be stressful.

One way we can support principals is to study effective schools and effective school leaders, identifying those attitudes, behaviors, and characteristics that create optimal learning environments and replicate them. Together we have served as educators for more than forty-five years in a variety of roles. Jeff has served as a teacher at all grade levels, assistant principal, principal, and central office administrator. Anthony has served as a high school teacher, assistant principal, principal, and central office administrator. Although all these roles required long hours and were, at times, quite stressful, we agree that the role of principal is perhaps the most challenging. One thing that helped us succeed as school principals was having a set of core leadership values (i.e., principles) to which we adhered consistently. Based on our own experiences as school administrators as well as our observations of school leaders in many other schools, we have found that most effective principals also lead according to principles they adhere to consistently. Some may have adopted these principles almost intuitively, while others may have adopted them over time through trial and error, but excellent school administrators lead as "principled principals." Almost everything they do is based on strongly held beliefs about what is best for their school community. Over time, such "principled principals" rarely need to waste time deliberating about what to do next or whether to initiate a new program. As the quote above suggests, principled principals have already decided how to act before they encounter the decision-making opportunity.

Those they lead come to realize this fact and take comfort in knowing the school is run on principle rather than by whimsy. Teachers become more confident in their leaders and become more confident in themselves, and this confidence is passed along to the students they teach.

Serving as a school principal is tough. It is the most demanding and challenging job we have had in our careers. At the same time, serving as school administrators is one of the most exciting and rewarding jobs. Although nothing we do or say will make the job of school principal an easy one, there are ways we can make it easier—and more rewarding.

Enduring Principles for Principals

We have met and worked with some outstanding school administrators across the country. Many of these professionals share their insights in subsequent chapters of this book. On the other hand, we have come across some principals who were decidedly less effective.

In studying the most successful school leaders we know, we've noticed many diverse traits. Some are quite charismatic, while others are almost reticent by nature. Some are veteran administrators, and others have served only a few years in the role. Some are from rural areas, while others serve in urban or suburban districts. Although they differ in many ways, they also share traits in common. None of these principals lead capriciously; instead, they lead with intention, meaning they have a set of values, standards, beliefs, and *principles* which guide them.

That's not to say they are rigid people who never deviate from the planned course of action or never act out of character, but it does mean they behave consistently, relying on these principles to guide their words and actions. Based on our research, the majority of these leaders do not actually have a formal list of guiding tenets written down anywhere, but we suspect they can share them verbally with anyone who asks.

When identifying the traits, behaviors, beliefs, and actions of our most successful school leaders, the list tends to go on and on; however, we have found that most fall into one of ten categories we call "Principal Principles." These principles will provide a framework for you to fast-track your growth as a leader and affirm areas where you're already on the right track.

Principle 1—The Priority Principle

Effective school principals understand and accept that anything involving the school they serve is important. As such, they make it their practice to communicate the message: "It's all important" to the school community—in particular, staff members they lead. Although they treat everything and everyone in the school as important, they also realize the need to prioritize the many competing demands upon their attention, intentionally making time to focus on each. They know what to start, stop, and continue doing and how to recognize what needs attention, when it needs attention, and whom to enlist to help lead the way. Effective principals prioritize the many important aspects of their job.

Principle 2—The People Principle

Effective school principals know that education is a "people first" endeavor and work intentionally to build positive relationships with everyone in the school community. They work extremely hard each day yet never forget the "fun factor," modeling for those around them that teaching, learning, and leading should be joyful enterprises. They are not afraid to share their thoughts and feelings with others. When they make a mistake, they admit they were wrong, apologizing and reflecting on what they learned so they can do better in the future. Effective principals realize that little in our noble profession is inherently "right" or "wrong" and allow others autonomy in how they accomplish goals.

Principle 3—The Self-Leadership Principle

Effective school principals are acutely aware that to lead others, they must first lead themselves. They are passionate not only about leading, but also learning, constantly trying to grow, learn, and share their learning with students, staff, and parents. They send the message to those they serve that they consider themselves a work in progress, continually experimenting and evolving on their quest to improve. They seek out people, opportunities, and resources that can help them get better so they can better serve others. Effective principals model lifelong learning and self-improvement.

Principle 4—The Outcomes Principle

Effective school principals know that results matter and hold themselves and others in their schools accountable for adding value to the social, emotional, and academic lives of the students they serve. They ask, "How will we know if we are making a difference?" and plan periodic assessments to elicit data which will inform both how they are doing as well as which steps they must take next. They analyze all student, classroom, and school data consistently and share these findings with staff members. When results show that the school is making a difference, they celebrate this with staff. When results are less than expected, they confront these facts openly, too, and collaborate with staff to improve. Effective principals embrace the challenge of achieving positive student, staff, and school outcomes.

Principle 5—The Talent Principle

Effective school principals know that effective teachers can have a profoundly positive impact on the students they teach. Knowing how important it is to have effective educators in place throughout the school, these principals take the hiring process very seriously, recruiting and hiring the very finest professionals they can find for every opening that arises in their building. They have intentional hiring practices in place that increase the likelihood of selecting individuals who will succeed once hired. Effective principals surround themselves with excellent people.

Principle 6—The Change Principle

Effective school principals welcome change, viewing it as an opportunity for growth. They realize not everyone in their school enjoys change. As a result, when initiating change, they work to address the hopes and fears of those involved in the change process. They realize our global society is changing at a furious pace and schools, too, must change in order to best prepare students for the twenty-first century and beyond. When leading change, these principals clearly explain why change is happening, whom it will affect, and how it will be carried out. Effective principals understand change is the one constant in schools today and never shy away from exploring new and better ways to do their work.

Principle 7—The Communication Principle

Effective school principals communicate frequently and intentionally with the students, staff, and parents they serve and, when in doubt, err on the side of over communicating. They realize the damage that can occur when members of the school community feel uninformed or "left out of the loop." They communicate in a variety of ways, using both traditional and innovative means to meet the needs of all stakeholders. They realize the power of stories and often communicate the messages they wish to send using powerful storytelling techniques. Effective principals never miss an opportunity to inform, inspire, celebrate, and challenge others through ongoing, strategic communication.

Principle 8—The Management Principle

Effective school principals are visionary leaders passionate about "big picture" plans for transforming the school experience for the students and staff they serve. At the same time, they are well aware that each day is filled with a host of less glamorous, but equally important, managerial or operational duties and responsibilities. Serving as a school principal at any level can be one of the most hectic jobs we know. Twelve-hour workdays swiftly become the norm rather than the exception. In such a fast-paced and task-filled atmosphere, it can be easy to inadvertently allow certain managerial tasks to fall through the cracks. Successful principals know how damaging this can be to the culture of a school and the extent to which such oversights can negatively impact bigger picture events. They therefore have in place systems for attending to every aspect of how the school runs. Although they perform many of these tasks themselves, they also enlist and empower others to help lead this important work. Effective school principals know that taking care of the "little" things makes it more likely they will accomplish the "big" things.

Principle 9—The Harmony Principle

Effective school principals relish professional debates which are conducted in a professional and respectful manner and encourage staff members to honestly let them know when they disagree with something or someone in the school. They are equally adamant about confronting—in a dignified and respectful manner—underperformance or behavior that is out of alignment with agreed-upon, shared values. In general, however, they are leaders who cultivate an atmosphere of harmony in the schoolhouse, establishing and maintaining an environment in which all people in the school go out of their way to be kind to one another. When stressful situations arise, these leaders maintain an aura of calm, modeling how they would like others to respond to the inevitable mini crises that occur. Effective school principals exude a sense of calm professionalism at all times—especially during times of conflict or crisis.

Principle 10—The Collaboration Principle

Effective school principals tend to be collaborative by nature and are definitely collaborative by design. They know school leadership is a team effort and rely on colleagues within the school and across the district to help move the school forward. Although they enjoy collaborating with others on a wide variety of school-related issues, they are not afraid to stand up for what they believe, even when such beliefs go against those of others on the team. In addition, although they will do anything in their power to help a colleague at another school get better, they also possess a competitive side, striving to be the very best at what they do so the schools they lead become recognized as among the very best. When collaborating with colleagues, effective school principals keep the focus on what works best for the kids they serve.

The 4 Cs for Principals

We suspect there is nary an educator serving today who has not heard about the 4Cs of twenty-first-century learning: *communication, creativity, collaboration,* and *critical thinking.* Our society will always need citizens who can speak, write, and listen effectively, who can generate new ideas and products, who can work well with their fellow citizens, and who can problem solve, analyze, and evaluate. Although we will never underestimate the importance of these "4 Cs," in order for them to develop in classrooms with increasing frequency, we need schools with positive, productive, learner-centered cultures.

School culture is perhaps the most important indicator of whether students, teachers, and schools will reach their potential. And the person with the greatest influence on school culture is the principal. The job of creating and maintaining a positive and productive school culture is so important that we call it Job #1 for the principal. In fact, the most important 4 Cs in the twenty-first century (and beyond) for school principals are: *culture, culture, culture,* and *culture.*

With the wrong school culture in place, the best we can ever hope for is pockets of excellence scattered throughout the building. With the right school culture in place, the sky is the limit for every student, every teacher, and every leader in the school community.

Peter Drucker is widely credited for saying that "organizational culture eats strategy for breakfast." We agree and believe this sentiment is especially true for our most important organization: our schools. Fortunately, influencing the school culture is something the school principal not only *should* do, but *can* do.

We recently surveyed twenty school administrators in one district asking them to list their top "culture crushers," those behaviors that can damage almost every aspect of the school. Here are a few that stood out as particularly harmful to school culture:

- When competition supersedes collaboration
- When inappropriate adult behavior goes unaddressed
- When teachers lose the desire to grow in their field
- When staff members do not understand the "why" of a decision
- Teachers who act as bullies to other teachers
- When leaders do not interact with their staff

- Teachers who cannot celebrate their colleague's success
- Assigning blame when something goes awry
- Focusing on petty issues and things that do not really matter in the big picture
- Lack of direction
- Lack of support
- Jealousy and cliques among colleagues
- Lack of trust between administrators and teachers
- Not having norms and expectations established for how to behave when difficult situations arise
- Adult-centered decisions driving how the school/district operates instead of doing what is best for students
- Using data to punish instead of using data to problem solve and ask questions
- Using the terms "I" and "you" versus "we" and "us"
- Satisfaction with the status quo
- Fixed mindsets
- Acceptance of poor performance
- Gossiping about colleagues, students, and families
- Staff members who say they will get on board with school initiatives but, behind closed doors, do not

We can see you nodding your head in agreement. Effective school leaders realize creating and maintaining a positive school culture is of paramount importance. They also realize school culture starts with them—and embrace that responsibility.

Whom This Book Is for and How to Use It

Throughout this book, we'll share our own stories as well as the stories of other educators we have come to know and respect. We will look at where excellent leaders focus their attention, how they spend their time and energy, what guides their decisions, and more importantly, how others can learn from them so all school leaders can grow.

We wrote this book, first and foremost, for current school administrators and aspiring school administrators. As former principals who each completed master's, specialist's, and doctoral programs in educational administration, we also wrote this book for university programs designed to prepare educators to succeed in the role of school principal. Although excellent books on school administration are currently available, we wanted to create a more practical work, grounded in actual experiences in the field.

We close each of the ten core chapters with our version of a 3-2-1 activity to tie it all together and reflect on the following:

3 Principal Perspectives on the Principle: In this section, we include the voice of three current principals who share their thoughts. We invited principals from across the country to share their thoughts on why the topic matters and what success looks like.

2 Resources Related to the Principle: In this section, we share two of our favorite resources for learning more about the chapter's focus.

1 Culture Crusher Related to the Principle: In this section, we include examples of how the principle under discussion is undermined in schools with a counterproductive school culture and how to avoid such pitfalls.

Thank you for joining us in our quest to learn more about what beliefs, behaviors, skills, and mindsets allow some principals to stand out and how we can help all school leaders continuously grow and improve. The job of school principal is physically, emotionally, and intellectually demanding. It is stressful and requires long hours of work on a daily basis. Principals are "on the clock" twenty-four hours a day, 365 days a year. The job comes with many burdens—and many rewards.

To succeed, principals need to stand on tried-and-true principles of excellence that guide them on their leadership journey. You are not alone in this journey. The ten principles and insights from experienced colleagues will equip you to positively transform your school.

PRINCIPLE 1
The Priority Principle

Everything is important; success is in the details.
—Steve Jobs

One of our favorite times of year is March. In the Chicago area, where we live, it means the long cold winter is almost over. But a more important reason to love March is because college basketball's March Madness is upon us. The NCAA basketball tournament is one of our favorite sporting events—a single-elimination tournament in which there can be only one champion. The team that comes out on top isn't always the one with the best offense or the best defense; rather, it's the team that plays both offense and defense well. All champions in the NCAA tournament as well as champions in other sports understand: when it comes to winning, it's *all* important.

But if it's *all* important, how do we decide where to focus our time and effort? What needs our attention and when? These are questions that often arise in schools regardless of the initiative or undertaking. Another question that pops up in schools happens to be one of the most counterproductive questions we ask: "Is that the most important thing we do?" If you are a principal, assistant principal, or a teacher, you've heard this question before, more than likely when confronting teachers or staff with student performance data. You may have even posed the question yourself.

Is that the most important thing we do? can be a deadly question to pose in our schools, and principals who answer it incorrectly commit a critical error.

The reason why is simple: It is all important. That's right; everything we do is important. In education we do not get to make distinctions that one thing is more important than another. How can we say that social-emotional learning is more important than reading or vice versa? When we ask and answer that question, we are doing nothing more than stating an individual opinion that is not supported by facts.

Everything we do is important.

In reality, students need our full commitment to everything we provide in schools. Schools should be in the business of developing well-rounded critical thinkers who are socially and emotionally prepared to be contributors in our society. In order for schools to embrace this concept, we need principals to believe every facet of education is important—and possible—to deliver.

We're well aware of the familiar mantra, "If everything is important, then nothing is important." We understand this sentiment and realize the need to juggle priorities. But in the noble profession of education, everything we provide—and every way we provide it—is important.

The False Dilemma

In philosophy there is a term called a "false dilemma." It is a type of logical fallacy where only two options are presented when, in actuality, more options exist. A clear example of the false dilemma is the phrase, "You are either with us or against us." There are only two choices presented, but there may be many more options.

In education, we seem to love the false dilemma; in fact, it's baked into the culture of many classrooms and systems. Consider the following common examples:

False Dilemmas in Education

- You pass or fail
- That answer is right or wrong
- Full credit or no credit
- Homework is complete or it's not done at all
- Either you support school choice, or you support failing schools

And on and on it goes.

The most damaging of these false dilemmas, however, is usually presented as a choice between several core areas of schools. Academics, social-emotional learning, and innovation come to mind as three areas we deem as equally important but are often asked to choose between. For example, a grade level that had poor academic growth for the school year might be very quick to ask, "But is ensuring academic growth the most important thing we do? The kids really loved school this year, and isn't that more important?"

It is important that kids like (or even love) school. But it is also important that they learn and grow. As principals, we cannot give in to the idea that there are some things in school more valued than others when, in fact, they should all be valued.

Another common example is the resistance from some to move from traditional to more innovative instructional practices. More than once we have heard the following statement: "I would love to do these cool, innovative activities in my classroom, but we have to be accountable for those darn test scores."

This statement is one of the most damaging in terms of its impact on innovation and student learning. Let's look at a clear example from the 2015 Partnership for Assessment for College and Career Readiness (PARCC) released items test questions. This is a public test practice item available on their website.

4. A patio is in the shape of a rectangle with a width of 8 feet and a length of 9 feet. What is the area? Enter your answer in the box.

[   ] square feet

Now, what is it about this question that tells educators they cannot teach creatively or implement innovative learning experiences that put students in charge of their learning? Would the best way to learn this content and answer this question successfully be to sit at a desk and listen to a lecture or engage in project-based learning and actually build things? And what about the above question would make someone think they couldn't have students blogging or using multimedia tools to explain their thinking and then share it with classmates?

Another counterproductive outcome of false-dilemma thinking is the devaluing of valid and reliable assessments of student learning. The more principals buy into this, the more damaging it becomes. Schools and classrooms are publicly touting a choice between twenty-first-century innovation and student learning. Devaluing academic learning and measurements of that learning is not the intention of innovation. But far too often, that is exactly what happens.

Only those living under a rock the past few years missed the uproar from both the education community and the general public over the new state assessments such as PARCC or Smarter Balanced, which were unveiled to align with the new state standards. There are numerous reasons given for why people are against standardized assessments, but we suspect it is less about testing and more about measuring student learning in the first place.

This is a simplistic example, but it makes the point. Teachers are not the sole purveyors of these false dilemmas; in fact, we hear just as many of these comments emanating from principals. One of the most important things a principal can do is not fall prey to this false choice. We must demonstrate to our teachers, parents, and students that it is *all* important, including measuring whether students are learning and prepared for the next steps of their journeys.

What Are the Most Important Things We Do?

If we take the time to do something in school, it should be important enough to do well; yet, there are areas that encompass the vast majority of what we do in school. These are often posed as either/or, false-dilemma choices. With the mindset of *it's all important,* let's examine three general areas of a school's responsibilities.

Social-Emotional Health and Learning

Social-emotional learning is crucial for students. We are not, after all, creating widgets. Our schools are the development centers for the next generation of scholars, leaders, CEOs, politicians, and... humans! We need to ensure these students and future leaders will grow up with a healthy dose of empathy and the ability to understand themselves and others. Aside from the mental health and societal benefits of social-emotional learning, students benefit from increased self-management and self-awareness. They become goal setters and, in turn, goal achievers. Research has also shown that social-emotional learning can have a positive impact on a student's academic performance as well.

In many schools, however, social-emotional learning is often subordinated in importance to academics. We can make the mistake of thinking schools doing well academically do not need strong social-emotional curricula. We cannot assume students naturally have these skills and dispositions. Students from all backgrounds must be taught life skills and preventative education around drugs and alcohol. They must have the opportunity to develop positive self-perceptions. It is up to us, as principals, to avoid the trap of false dilemmas and instead champion social-emotional health *and* learning as a non-negotiable component of our schools.

Academics

Another major area of importance in schools is, obviously, academic learning. Research has shown that many students who are not reading proficiently by the end of third grade do not graduate from high school on time. According to the Annie E. Casey Foundation (2012), every student who does not graduate high school costs our society $260,000 in lost earnings, taxes, and productivity. For students who eventually graduate from high school and go on to college, there are other costs to not being properly prepared. Approximately one in four students graduating high school today require remedial classes during their first year in college. This is not just inconvenient, it also costs almost $1.5 billion per year for students and their families. When principals look at K–2 students, they should view this period as the most important educational years of students' lives. How they grow in these early grades will lay the foundation for all future learning.

As harsh as it sounds, it is simply not enough for students to feel good about school. We want them to enjoy school, of course, but they must also learn, and we must commit to this outcome as a professional guarantee we offer every child we serve. To accomplish this goal, we need excellent teachers. A poor teacher can set a child back a year or more in their learning and potentially create a gap so vast it becomes nearly impossible to catch up with peers.

One of the most important jobs of the principal is to ensure students are learning and growing. This is done in many ways, including monitoring teaching, ensuring a guaranteed and viable curriculum, and maintaining a positive school culture. But it is first and foremost accomplished by never compromising the fact that learning needs to happen. Results do matter.

When students do not learn and grow, teachers, principals, and school systems tend to look at any and every possible cause but themselves. "It's the test, the lack of funding, the kids, or their parents." And while lack of funding and resources are real problems to overcome, successful principals never let them become an excuse. Our students will be negatively impacted at some point if they are not learning. It is up to us to insist on learning as a non-negotiable in our schools.

Innovation

We are preparing students for jobs that do not even exist in today's society. Many of the in-demand jobs today were not even in existence ten years ago. This is just one of many reasons to foster innovation in our schools. George Couros aptly defines innovation as "something both new and better." This does not necessarily mean technology, although it can be included; rather, it means doing something you have not done before or doing it better—with an improvement of some sort. Innovating, in order to change outdated school practices for new generations of learners, is one of the most important things we can do as principals. There is no excuse for *not* innovating.

There is no excuse for *not* innovating.

We love speaking with principals who are reimagining their learning spaces—regardless of their resources. These makerspaces, STEM labs, or even reimagined libraries allow teachers and students to explore concepts in hands-on, project-based learning environments. When first looking for ways to innovate, a school library is a great place to start. If you are still teaching encyclopedia skills . . . stop! You will have taken your first step toward innovation in your library. Yes, the school library is a special place, but it's also one of the spots becoming more and more outdated for our students. If you look at new community libraries, they look nothing like most school libraries. The furniture and layout of all the spaces has changed with the times. It's time all schools follow suit.

Another way we see great principals pushing for innovation in their schools is to rethink the furniture in classrooms. When it is time to replace desks and chairs, many great principals we know are opting for tables rather than desks so students can collaborate more readily. They also have begun to abandon the idea of having a "front of the room" and a "back of the room." (By the way, this rearrangement of desks costs exactly zero dollars.) The entire environment is being redesigned to support learning. In these classrooms, lessons begin to reflect the new design of the learning environment, and student collaboration becomes the norm, not the exception.

If you are not at the point of replacing furniture or upgrading facilities, look to instruction as the place where innovation can have the most impact. Nearly all schools now have some form of technology available. Not all schools may be a 1:1 learning environment with each student having their own device, but we'd be willing to bet there are more than a couple of iPads or Chromebooks in nearly every school. Ask yourself how these are used. Are they used to change the learning experience or just transfer the old experience to a digital form?

Consider, for example, Kindergarten students learning a letter sound. In a more traditional setting, children would sit at their desks and complete worksheets on which they drew a line from the letter to the appropriate picture. What if, instead of the worksheet, the assignment was to grab an iPad and explore the classroom? When the student found an item that made the specific letter sound, they could take a photo of it, then record a video pronouncing the word and upload it directly to their teacher for feedback. This subtle shift in accomplishing a learning goal is a simple example of innovative learning.

Are teachers using technology in this way? Can they? It is up to us as principals to prioritize innovation as a non-negotiable in our schools.

Urgency and Importance

As principals, we set the tone for our schools, our staff, our students, and our community about what is important. Education is perhaps the largest human resource industry in the world. Every day, we are doing nothing less than preparing the doctors, nurses, scientists, and artists to succeed in a changing world. What are the skills they will need? Good habits and sense of self? Of course. A strong academic foundation? Absolutely. An ability to work with others, think flexibly, and innovate? You bet. These are all important, and we are wise to not rank them in importance.

Author Patrick Lencioni suggests that if everything is important, then nothing is. This is sound advice, particularly when focusing on what to prioritize in a day, a week, or even a month. But in the sense of our school or the academic year as a whole, we cannot become trapped by the false dilemma. The stakes are too high for our students. Remember, it's all important. If something we do is not a priority, we should not be doing it.

Have To's versus Must Do's

When we were growing up, we both had to take out the garbage regularly. We also had to help with the dishes, clean our rooms, mow the lawn, and sweep out the garage. We were raised by parents who loved and cared about us and who also expected us to help out with the daily household chores. These were our "Have To's." At the same time, those who raised us also believed that we should play outside often, ride our bikes, join athletic teams, go to the library, and even take occasional family trips to the local ice cream shop. It was equally important to the people raising us that we enjoy these types of activities. These became our "Must Do's," the things we were truly passionate about and looked forward to.

As principals, we found that life didn't change much. We still had "Have To's" and "Must Do's" and we found they were both important. Some of our daily, weekly, monthly, and annual tasks were more enjoyable than others, but just like taking out the garbage and going to the ice cream shop, we realized both were important. Creating annual crisis plans, budget reports, and dealing with student misbehavior were just a few of our "Have To's." Visiting classrooms every day, taking time to engage in the occasional kickball game, and celebrating student and teacher accomplishments were our professional "Must Do's."

We suspect that most everyone's personal and professional lives are filled with a balance of "Have To's" and "Must Do's." In education, the most successful principals we know understand that the "Have To's" are every bit as important as the "Must Do's." Some things are important because we have to do them to operate safely and efficiently. Although no one enjoys tornado drills, we have to prepare for a potential threat to our safety no matter how remote. None of us would suggest that we skip this important task despite its relative unpleasantness. On the other hand, other things are important because we simply *must* do them to fulfill our professional passion. Comforting a crying youngster, meeting with a troubled parent, and celebrating our successes are but a few examples of "Must Do's" in our schools.

If we tried to list every single duty, responsibility, and task expected of a school principal, it would consume the remainder of this book—and half your library. But specifically, in "The Big 3" of social-emotional learning, academic achievement, and innovative teaching and learning, we must lead with the clear message that we cannot choose one over another.

The Priority Principle
3–2–1

3

PRINCIPALS' PERSPECTIVES ON THE PRIORITY PRINCIPLE

Derek McCoy (@mccoyderek) is principal of West Rowan Middle School in Rowan-Salisbury Schools in North Carolina. He's an award-winning leader committed to helping schools improve learning and teaching by changing mindsets and skill sets of all stakeholders. Derek knows that in order to accomplish this goal, he must adeptly manage wide-ranging tasks and responsibilities on a daily basis. Derek occasionally feels conflicted when others suggest school leaders should only focus on one or two things:

> I've always been very attentive to advice given to me by my mentors and supervisors, not because I want to necessarily emulate their thinking and actions, but I want the best for my students, teachers, school, and school community. The principal's job responsibilities are tremendous, and I try to remain humble, remembering that others have been here before. Personal and professional advice, through a book or live coaching, is a gift I accept readily.
>
> One piece of advice I have always struggled with has been to focus on one or two things and make that your priority without

letting anything distract you. Then, when that is accomplished, move on to the next priority.

My goal, like all my mentors and supervisors, is to positively affect the learning and teaching in my school while enriching the lives of all stakeholders. On any given day, that will mean many different things, not one or two things:

- Hosting parent meetings to discuss changes in student work
- Designing ongoing professional learning with teachers to help shift thinking and practices around the topic of grading and assessment
- Developing and maintaining effective means of communication with students, staff, and parents
- Sharing best practices in communicating with parents and guardians to ensure we are building good partnerships

We can backwards-connect actions and plans to several big goals, but it's impossible for school leaders focused on building up the school, community, teaching, and learning not to remain focused on all these things. Our success comes from building capacity in our teams and colleagues to ensure that all students win in the end. Serving as an effective principal does require that I juggle many tasks, and at times, I must prioritize which to focus on. I will always have to circle back, however, to a multitude of other priorities at some other time. We cannot just do one thing well; we must do all things well.

Jenny Nauman (@PrincipalNauman) is a 2016 National Distinguished Principal of the 2013 National Blue Ribbon School, Shields Elementary, in the Cape Henlopen School District in Lewes, Delaware. Jenny has served as an administrator for a decade and was previously a second- and third-grade teacher and a reading specialist. Jenny knows that focusing on the most important task at any given moment while also keeping a multitude of other important priorities on her radar is challenging, yet achievable:

> Being an administrator of a K–5 school with 750 students is a challenging and rewarding profession. Understanding how to manage the multitude of "must do's" for a school year (or even a day) can be overwhelming. I often ask the question, "How do I focus on the most important thing while still keeping everything that is important a priority?" The answer isn't easy, but it is achievable.
>
> We know all the things we do in a school—from making sure everyone is safe to ensuring that our students have the best curriculum and instruction—are all necessary components of a successful school. It is all important, but we also have to remember that complexity is the enemy of implementation. How do we keep it simple, ensure that it all gets done, and, most importantly, make sure that what's best for our students is always at the forefront? At Shields, our successes are directly related to carefully juggling the following:
>
> - *Collaboration with School Improvement Team*—With this team, I work to see what's worked and what has not. We discuss what's been best for our students. We decide on areas that no longer need strong support and areas that still need our focus and support; for example, we have focused on Number Talks for many years in math. This will continue to be a priority but not one we need to focus on every day, as it is something that is now part of our culture.
>
> - *Creation of a Dashboard*—We create a dashboard to keep our eyes on everything. Safety is always at the top of the list, and we are sure to share the plan with all. The same goes for our expectations for instruction and our curriculum maps. While all subjects are important, some years have different areas of academic focus. That doesn't mean we forget about the rest; for example, this coming year we will be implementing a new literacy program. While math, science, and social studies will still be on our dashboard, reading will be a top priority.

- *Monitoring Progress*—The most important aspect of prioritizing is monitoring the established priorities along with
everything else. As a leader, the best way to ensure that
the priorities are being met is to be VISIBLE. By walking the
halls, going into classrooms, and conducting walk-throughs,
you can quickly check the pulse of the school as it relates
to your goals; for example, each month during the School
Improvement Team meeting, we spend between five and ten
minutes discussing and refocusing our energies. Delegating
the monitoring to team leaders helps save time. Overall, this
helps ensure that what's best for our school and all our students is at the forefront.

Personally, I write a to-do list each week (sometimes each
day) to help me stay focused. Writing these lists helps me plan
and organize my week to ensure that I can be out of my office
interacting with students and teachers as much as possible.
Collaborate with your best people, create a dashboard, and monitor continually in order to keep your school in check!

Mark McCord (@MarkMccord10) is principal of Stockdick
Junior High in Katy, Texas. He is a servant leader who finds
joy in the success of others. In 2016 he was selected as the
Katy ISD Secondary Principal of the Year. As principal of a very
large junior high school, Mark juggles a multitude of important
responsibilities. No matter how busy he gets, he never over-
looks the importance of being in classrooms and responding
to students, staff, and parents who need him at a moment's
notice. Somehow Mark manages to get it all done and shares
just a bit about how he does so here:

At my core, I deeply value service and contribution. Serving
in the role of principal allows me multiple opportunities to act
upon these values. The sheer number of opportunities can over-
whelm me as I push to do the work that I am motivated to do

while balancing everything else. My priority as the principal is to support and build capacity in my teachers. I understand that this is my zone of greatest influence. As the instructional leader, this involves teacher development through coaching. When I don't make time to get into classrooms to give my teachers the feedback they crave, I realize I've lost focus on where I can make the greatest impact for students.

One might ask how I accomplish this when everything is of importance. My greatest ally in this battle for balance is my professional calendar and the discipline to adhere to it.

Every task that needs to be accomplished is set on my calendar, including my coaching days. My goal each week is to have two full days acting as a coach by observing my staff and giving feedback. More often than not, I schedule four half-days to accommodate appointments. My focus on these days is to be in classrooms, meet directly with teachers, or provide feedback electronically. This strategy has allowed me to visit classrooms hundreds of times during the year as an investment in my teacher's growth through personal feedback.

The calendar is also my friend when it comes to completing the many other tasks. A strategy I employ is scheduling time on my calendar to reflect on district meetings. During this time, I dig into my notes and any other materials provided at the meeting to determine the actions I need to take. This purposeful dive into the information ensures that I meet the expectations laid out for me and allows me to work efficiently.

If you are currently sitting in the principalship, you realize that simply putting something on the calendar does not make it happen. Action only occurs through discipline and commitment. I never regret when I have to move things down the calendar to support the relational side of our work. Supporting a student, family, or staff member in crisis takes precedence over everything else. What sets effective leaders apart is the commitment to revisit the calendar and reschedule our important work when this happens.

2

PRIORITY PRINCIPLE RESOURCES

For a list of these and other resources, please visit theprincipledprincipal.com.

"The Big Rocks: Priority Management for Principals"
In this article, Kim Marshall identifies ten "Big Rocks" for principals and strategies for staying focused on the many important priorities in our schools.

"Stephen Covey's Time Management Matrix Explained"
In this blog post, Steve Mueller takes a look at Covey's "Urgent-Important" matrix and explains how this time management grid can help you manage your available time more efficiently.

1

PRIORITY PRINCIPLE
CULTURE CRUSHER

Whenever we allow a staff member to not follow through on any current initiative, we are destroying the culture at that school.

Whether that initiative is a school advisory program, a testing plan, a 1:1 technology implementation, standing in the hallways during transition times, or a myriad of other possibilities, if it is important enough to do, it is important that everyone in the school commits to doing it with 100 percent consistency. It is simply not acceptable for certain teachers to opt out of anything the school has decided to implement. Although effective principals allow teachers a great deal of autonomy, they also establish certain non-negotiables and hold everyone at the school accountable.

When a staff member fails to behave accordingly, principled principals do not look the other way; they act swiftly and decisively. They meet with the staff member privately to learn why the behavior occurred and to ensure it changes. In such meetings, they often follow four simple steps:

1. **Explain**—Principled principals clearly explain why they are concerned, pointing out specific examples of behaviors they deem as counter to agreed-upon behaviors.

2. **Ask**—They seek to understand the staff member's perspective, including whether the person agrees with their assessment of the situation and why they are acting as

they are. They ask probing questions and sincerely listen to their colleague's responses.

3. **Remind**—They remind the staff member why the issue is important to the success of the school as well as their expectations for all staff members to commit.

4. **Next**—Principled principals recap the meeting by clearly outlining next steps and inviting the staff member to offer his or her own solutions and goals for moving forward.

Holding all staff members accountable for following through on school standards is one way we build the culture of the school. When we address underperformance, we can earn trust, increase our credibility, and validate the efforts of everyone in the school who is doing the right thing.

PRINCIPLE 2
The People Principle

No one cares how much you know, until they
know how much you care.
—Theodore Roosevelt

The principal should be the model for how all other individuals in the school community act and how they treat each other. These relationships include all stakeholders within a school community: teachers, students, and parents.

The principal sets the tone and expectations, not by words, but by actions. As our friend Todd Whittaker says, "When the principal sneezes, the whole school catches a cold." We think the same can be said about a contagious smile. The people principle and all the practices associated with it apply to everyone with whom the leader interacts—and affects how teachers, parents, and students interact with each other. Good practices are good practices regardless of whom we are with at the moment. When we focus on building positive relationships, we do it on a human level and with heart.

How leaders act as human beings, not just as school leaders, is the key to the people principle. Here are some practical reminders:

Exhibit Empathy

Empathy is essential to all our relationships. We have to be able to put ourselves into the past, present, and future shoes of those we lead in order to truly understand them. If we cannot truly understand where people are coming from and what is important to them, we cannot lead them.

One of the first things we tell new teachers is how important "parent communication" is for their success; however, we don't mean newsletters or emails, although these should be part of our communication plan. What we mean is the importance of how the teacher shows love and care to each child in their classroom. Anytime a parent walks into a teacher's classroom or a principal's office with a problem, the one thing they want to know is whether we *care* about their child. As school leaders, we must never forget this.

If we cannot truly understand where people are coming from, we cannot lead them.

Although seemingly obvious, we must always remember that our students are the most important beings in the world to their parents. To a parent, these are not merely "students," and we have yet to meet a parent who does not want what's best for his or her child. The children who rarely sit still, who blurt out when they aren't supposed to, or who are frequently late with assignments are still the most special person alive in their parents' eyes. So when parents sit across from us with a problem, they are not looking for educational jargon, procedural policies, or even promises that we will make everything better. They are looking for reassurance that we also care about their child.

The fact that this is so important should be good news because empathy and caring are within our control. It would be wonderful to promise parents that nothing will ever go wrong and that every day will be full of successful learning experiences—social, emotional, and academic growth, with nary a negative peer interaction along the way. But life, of course, does not work that way, nor do our schools. Although we cannot promise a perfect day, we can promise to care and show others how much we care. This is the foundation from which we begin to solve all problems.

Much is written about the accomplishments and leadership of President Abraham Lincoln. Lincoln, like many other successful leaders, possessed a quality that so many often overlook. This quality is empathy.

In her book *Team of Rivals*, Doris Kearns Goodwin writes that Lincoln was uncommonly tenderhearted. The melancholy that he was known for came from his sensitivity to the pains and injustices he saw in the world. Lincoln is just one example of many leaders throughout history whose impact was increased by his ability to empathize with people on a deep level. We may be exposing our professional bias, but we believe leading a school is every bit as important as leading a nation. Although the comparison may be debatable, the idea that empathy is vital to relationship-building is clear.

A key to empathy is treating people as unique individuals. Great principals know they do not have a "staff"; instead, they have a team of human beings who happen to be staff members within the school. In addition to these human beings, the principal also leads hundreds or even thousands of students and parents. Great principals understand these people are not groups or categories; they are individuals, each with their own dreams, aspirations, struggles, and conflicts.

Consider an elementary school with fifty total "staff" members. At any given time in a busy school year, there can be numerous personal and professional issues occurring in the lives of these individuals. It is likely someone's close family member is struggling with a critical illness. Someone may have just learned they have cancer. Another person may be going through a divorce, while still another is struggling with one of their children. The first step to putting yourself in someone else's shoes is realizing that each individual is going through something unique to them. Committing to being an empathetic person is the foundation of the people principle. Principled principals lead with empathy.

Listen Intentionally

One way we can be more empathetic as leaders is to become better listeners. Before we can propose solutions or even begin the problem-solving process, we must actively listen to those we serve.

Although this may seem painfully obvious, we have witnessed many school leaders immediately jump in with solutions, answers, and ideas without first making the time to fully understand the situation and the multiple perspectives of those involved. We all know the feeling of not being "heard." We suspect that everyone has experienced this at some point.

When explaining something to a doctor, a spouse, a friend, or even a boss, we see their facial features begin to tighten as they proceed to interrupt us. They believe they understand our issue and proceed to enlighten us with their solution. Instead of simply sharing a situation, we're forced to either correct their inaccurate understanding or retreat from the conversation.

Although it can be tempting in the midst of an action-packed school day to jump right to the "solution" and move on to the next issue, principled principals make the time to treat each situation as unique—and requiring their full attention. Effective leaders listen patiently to everyone until they have a clear understanding of the issue. They listen not only to respond but also to understand. We cannot help people when we do not accurately understand their problem.

In thinking about the school leaders we consider excellent listeners, we realized that each of these professionals employ—knowingly or not—two simple techniques: First, they resist any temptation to interrupt. This is not rocket science, yet it seems to be the exception rather than the rule in conversations today. When we are listening, it should be about us understanding what the other person is saying. Let people finish. Second, skilled listeners seek clarity by repeating a summary of what has been said to ensure it was understood accurately. It is much better to clarify details *prior* to problem-solving.

Another key to effective listening is to understand *why* you are listening, and this is where empathy is so important. When you finally understand a person, you then must determine what they need from you. There are certainly times when someone will come into your office with a problem, hoping you can provide a solution, yet there are other times when they simply need you to listen. They may need you to be there for them on a professional level, but they may also need your active listening

39

on a personal level. Sometimes simply listening is one of the kindest acts we can do for another person. We need not offer our opinion, but we must find out what they expect from us. Principled principals are excellent listeners.

Show You Care

Great school leaders can never find enough opportunities to show they care about educators, students, parents, and others in the school community. And great principals make sure to create these opportunities whenever they can. Letting people know you care can take several forms, but all are manifestations of your words and actions.

Your words can stick people for a long time. Both of us vividly recall several statements—kind and unkind—from our own teachers and principals as we went through school. Whenever we speak, even "off the top of our heads," our words carry a lot of weight. Great principals monitor their spoken and written words, ensuring the amount of positive words emanating from them far outweighs the negative. Fortunately, there are unlimited ways to build others up with your words, and many of them are very simple.

One way is to write a personal note to every child in your school. Or better yet, write it to their parents. Set a goal to write at least two a day, and before you know it, you will have written to most of the students and families in your school. Great principals make this a habit. There is always enough time for the important. We suggest writing these at the start of your workday.

One principal relayed a powerful story of the impact this gesture can have. Early into the school year, a fourth-grade student was having a lot of difficulty with other kids at recess. The student often found his way into the principal's office where they would talk about what happened and discuss consequences for his behavior. One day while visiting his classroom, the principal noticed that the child was working hard on a project and helping other kids along by sharing his learning with them. The principal immediately wrote a note to the child and his parents describing how well he was working in the classroom and how lucky the school was to have him as a student.

The principal gave the boy the note in a sealed envelope and told him to go home and open it with his parents. Of course, the boy's first response was "Is it good?" as he recalled times the principal had previously spoken with his parents about problems the boy was having. The principal told the boy not to worry. The boy never said anything about the note to the principal, and they never discussed it again.

Fast forward more than a year and a half, when the boy was about to finish fifth grade. At a school meeting, the boy's mom told the principal that her son still had the note posted on his bedroom wall. Our words and actions can have a significant impact on others. It took very little time to write that note and even less time to notice the student's effort, but the impact of that action continued to sustain the young boy and his mother a year and a half later.

Our words and actions can have a significant impact on others.

Whenever you see a staff member doing something remarkable, let them know about it. Don't be afraid to say it, but even more importantly, show them you care enough to write it down and send it to them. This lets the person know you appreciate the great things they are doing, and it further encourages them to keep reinforcing a positive culture.

You can always take it a step further, with an idea we first learned from Todd Whitaker, by creating holiday greeting cards with a picture of the staff member on the front of the card. The handwritten message inside should express appreciation and center on how lucky the school is to have them serving there. Remember to include teachers, paraprofessionals, custodians, nurses, and food service workers. For added impact, consider mailing the cards directly to the homes of the staff members' parents—or their spouse or significant other. What kind of feeling would a card like that from the school principal have on the parents of a twenty-something child who has only been teaching for a couple of years? Or what about the elderly parents of a thirty-year veteran who receive this message about their child?

Just like our students, our staff members are also the most important people in the world to someone else. The best principals we know are always finding ways to make people working in the school feel special.

There are also less direct ways to show you care, and often we overlook them because we are so involved in following policies and contracts. Take, for instance, a staff member who needs to leave early one day for some reason. As principals, we all experience this. It's a Wednesday morning and a staff member comes to you asking if they can leave school twenty minutes before the contractual time because they have an appointment. What is your response?

As principals, we both found every opportunity to say "yes" to requests such as these. If it were at all possible and did not endanger students for a teacher to leave a few minutes early, it was always our goal to accommodate them. Yet many principals we know will categorically deny such requests to the point that no one will ever ask—which may be the reasoning behind their approach. These leaders often believe they are setting a poor precedent: If they let one person do it, they will be inundated with similar requests from others. To them, the teacher contract is clear about the working hours, and they stick to the contract language at all costs. And there are costs.

Remember what we said about not knowing what people are going through? What if someone is waiting on the results of a biopsy to determine if they have cancer, and the only time they can get an appointment is at the end of the school day? What if the child care center where a teacher sends her kids called and said her child was sick and needed to be picked up? As the principal, do you really want your response to be "Well, you will have to take a half day if you want to leave early"?

Both of us, on more than one occasion, have covered a teacher's class at the end or beginning of the day to help a person out. The reason we do such things is because of the people principle. We know that some principals may be worried about being taken advantage of, and there will be times that someone tries to take advantage of you. You cannot control *them*, but you can control *yourself.*

When we base our decisions on the people principle, we help people from a sincere place.

People generally want to do the right thing. When we base our decisions on the people principle, we help people from a sincere place. Over time, people appreciate it and even go the extra mile not to abuse professional courtesies. Yes, these attitudes build culture and loyalty. But effective principals do not act in such ways to build school culture and staff loyalty. They do so from a place of empathy and genuine care for the people they lead. That is the people principle in action.

Black and White . . . or Gray?

Great principals who understand the people principle know that things are rarely black and white. Lasting success, and a culture in which everyone cares about their work and each other, is never achieved by binary thinking. Don't get us wrong: Some issues in schools must absolutely be black and white. One of them is student safety. Another is student learning. But the example of an employee asking to leave early for an appointment shows how operating in the "gray" area brings success. Principals who decide to live by the union contract should also be prepared to die by the contract. Successful school cultures and professional relationships are never achieved in the strict language of a contract; they are found among the spaces in between. Operating in the gray area means making decisions based on a "people first" mindset.

> ### Operating in the gray area means making decisions based on a "people first" mindset.

Your willingness to think and operate in this way will absolutely change your school's culture. A leader we know recounted a lesson from her first year as principal. By many accounts, the principal before her had been very "black and white." No one ever left early. Whenever a teacher raised an issue of any type, the first thing to come out was a copy of the teachers' collective bargaining agreement. After our colleague became principal, the approach to these scenarios changed. Decisions became largely based on people, not necessarily predetermined by contract or policy language. The gray area was seen as a place to extend success, not somewhere to be avoided. The choice was to believe in people and treat them as human beings.

At this same school, an afternoon teacher "duty" was bus supervision. Teachers rotated weeks, making sure all students boarded the buses and the buses departed safely. One autumn, a major construction project near the school caused the buses to be delayed every day for almost half the school year. Sometimes buses did not leave school until thirty minutes after the school day was over, but teachers were only contractually obligated to stay at school ten minutes after the end of the day. Once the staff saw that their new principal treated them as people and was more than willing to cover their class for ten minutes or be an extra set of hands in their classroom whenever they needed it, they were also willing to help out when they didn't "have to."

In fact, during this time, the principal only received one complaint about having to stay late for bus duty. She was in the office after school that day with some teachers, including the school's union representative. A voice came through the walkie-talkie asking for the principal or assistant principal to relieve them at bus duty since they didn't "have to be here." The teacher had just returned from a leave of absence and assumed they were operating under the same rigid paradigm from the previous year.

The union representative was embarrassed, and everyone was surprised by the teacher's black-and-white attitude. Of course, the principal obliged and relieved the staff member, but she never heard another peep from that staff member or anyone else about extra bus duty responsibilities. We suspect there may have been a conversation between the union representative and the newly returned teacher after the incident. Perhaps the representative said something like this: "We treat one another like people now; you don't have to act that way anymore."

Treating others the way you would like to be treated not only helps the other person, but it also helps you become a better leader. But more than that, it helps promote a positive school culture. The success of our school's culture is not found in the black and white. It is found in the gray.

Be Vulnerable

None of us are perfect—least of all the authors of this book. While we have both led successful schools, we have also made more than our fair share of mistakes. In such instances, one of the best things we can do for others is to be vulnerable: admit when things aren't going well, an idea didn't work, or a plan never came to fruition.

The perception that the principal should be an infallible professional leads some people to believe that, if the principal were to acknowledge a mistake, it is an admission of incompetence. Nothing could be further from the truth. The first thing "people principals" understand is when something does not go as planned, they will not be the only ones to know. Chances are, everybody knows. So when they do make mistakes or have an idea go awry, they reflect on it and own up to it—swiftly and publicly.

This honest vulnerability serves several purposes. First, it allows us to model reflection and acceptance of failure as a means to improvement and growth. There is almost nothing more frustrating than leaders who preach to teachers about accepting feedback on evaluations as a means to get better but fail to practice what they preach. Principals are every bit as much in need of feedback and reflection about their practice as anyone else. Owning up to a mistake—or an idea that failed—allows people to see what the process of reflection, accountability, and perseverance looks like.

A second benefit of professional vulnerability is that when we model acceptance and ownership, we are helping facilitate that as part of our school culture. If it is acceptable for the leader to admit mistakes, then it's not only fine for teachers and other staff to do likewise, it's actually encouraged. By being personally vulnerable when things do not go right, we may actually help our school become that place where teachers truly reflect on practice and seek feedback.

A third benefit of serving as a vulnerable leader is a self-focused one. Admitting mistakes, saying we are sorry, reflecting, and moving on lifts a big weight off us as leaders. Not unlike what we teach our students, when we own and apologize for our mistakes, we immediately feel better and can move on to remedy the situation. Otherwise we must attempt to keep up the facade of perfection—a facade everyone can easily see through.

When we own and apologize for our mistakes, we immediately feel better and can move on to remedy the situation.

These mistakes and missteps do not have to be monumental or directly related to school. They can be personal, small, and even silly. For example, one principal told us about a time he put on two mismatched shoes one morning and only realized it as he entered the school. It had been a very busy morning at home. The shoes had been sitting near each other in his closet and, at some point, had been placed next to each other. As he walked into the office, he noticed many teachers and staff congregating in the office. It was too late to turn back home, so he went with it.

No one may have noticed, but when he came into the office and someone asked how he was, he replied, "Everything's going great . . . except my shoes." Everyone in the office had a good laugh, including the principal. This is a simple example, but we know people who would have been embarrassed about such a silly mistake and missed an opportunity to share a self-deprecating laugh with colleagues. People principals do not expect perfection from those they lead or from themselves. They model vulnerability as a way to grow.

Have Fun

One of the great things about the mixed-up shoe story is that the principal did not take himself too seriously. He took an opportunity to laugh with the staff in the office, and throughout the rest of the day, it became a point of smiling and laughter with staff and students. Schools should be fun places. As educators, we do some of the most important work in the world, and we need to approach our mission with seriousness. But the best way to achieve our mission is not with the demeanor of a drill sergeant, and we must never forget the fun-factor when serving in schools.

Great principals find opportunities to laugh with their colleagues, students, and families. They are masters at self-effacing humor and do not take themselves too seriously. They may spend time in dunk tanks, sing karaoke, and put themselves in a thousand other mildly embarrassing situations—while appearing to love every minute.

A principal wears many hats and plays many different roles. One of them is serving as the "ambassador of fun" (And no, this title is probably not written in black and white in your contract, either).

Look for opportunities to laugh with people in your school community.

We often hear about the need to make learning fun. The principal has the opportunity to help make learning—and working—fun for the students and staff they serve. The best principals we know consider this not only an opportunity but a professional responsibility. Does this mean that you should start taking comedy classes? Not at all. Simply look for opportunities to laugh with people in your school community. Don't take yourself so seriously. And allow yourself, your colleagues, your students, and your school as a whole to consider a lively sense of humor an important aspect of the school culture.

The People Principle
3–2–1

3

PRINCIPALS' PERSPECTIVES ON THE PEOPLE PRINCIPLE

Jessica Cabeen (@JessicaCabeen) is the principal of the Woodson Kindergarten Center in Austin, Minnesota. She is the 2017 Minnesota National Distinguished Principal and the 2016 National Association of Elementary School Principals (NAESP) Digital Leader of Early Learning. Jessica knows the importance of focusing on people first and doing the "small" things each day to ensure the people she serves are at the center of everything she does:

> Leading the only school in the district that serves every kindergarten student brings a great deal of pressure. As principal, I only have 174 days to invite, inspire, involve, and help educate over 350 students and their families. If I don't get it right—if I don't set the table correctly that year—I make it difficult for any other educator to change the trajectory of a family's perceptions of the school and those who serve inside it.
>
> A People's Principal has to lead from their feet, not from their seat. My mantra is "If serving is beneath you, leading is beyond you," and that is how I lead each and every day.

On this journey, I have learned that making intentional connections with people, if only for minutes a day, can go a long way. One of the ways I accomplish this commitment is by leading from the location of morning bus and parent drop off. For other principals, this may be a time for meetings, checking email, or talking with staff. For me, this is an opportunity to show parents, students, and school professionals that my priorities are where my feet are: with them, inside, outside, every day, rain or shine, sleet or snow. This small gesture has made a huge impact on those I serve and those who serve with me.

When building trusting relationships in a school that has over twenty-five different home languages represented, a smile, hug, high-five, or handshake is easily translated. Actions show "by all means possible, we will provide their children with an incredible school day." Some days I am learning the Cupid Shuffle with a group of moms after taking multiple selfies with students coming off one of our school buses. Other days I am wearing the crossing guard jacket and moonwalking while moving parents forward in the car drop-off line. Occasionally I might even be in a family car encouraging and supporting a sad student who's saying goodbye to mom for the day.

Yes, as this type of a leader, you become more like family and less "official" with each passing day. I hear comments from families, like "My principal never greeted me like this every day" or "Thanks for really knowing who my child is at this school." An unexpected outcome of this work in building relationships is the enhanced trust and respect I receive from the school staff. Leading from the trenches, shoveling snow, wearing garbage bags as ponchos, or walking with a sad student as they come inside shows the staff where my priorities are and where to find me: with our families. What have I learned from this unconventional commitment to leading? Never doubt the daily gestures you make to build relationships. In the end, it amounts to so much more.

Amy Fadeji (@mrsfadeji) is principal of Penngrove Elementary in Petaluma, California. In her sixth year as principal, she continues to find herself reaching out to educators across the country to build a growing network of innovative and inspiring colleagues. After attending California Polytechnic San Luis Obispo and The University of Southern Mississippi, Amy taught second and third grades for seven years in Mobile, Alabama, and San Anselmo, California, before launching her career in administration. Amy finds great joy spending her days supporting students and teachers in their learning adventures. She is passionate about modeling and encouraging risk-taking and fostering collaboration, and she delights in helping other administrators and teachers do the same. She keeps people at the heart of everything she does as a school leader:

> As an elementary school principal, the only way I know how to lead is by keeping people at the heart of every single thing I do. Whether it's connecting with a student who needs a pep talk, supporting a teacher by running an intervention group, checking in with a parent who has been feeling uneasy, or making time to attend community events, there is no denying that this work revolves around people.
>
> Building lasting and authentic relationships is absolutely and without a doubt my favorite part about this job. When you truly take the time to get to know your students, staff, parents, and community members, everything becomes more meaningful. Celebrations suddenly take on a whole new life, hardships are blanketed with indescribable amounts of empathy, teaching and learning becomes filled with risk-taking and laughter, and an entire school community shifts its focus on what truly matters: people. Here are some of the best ways I know to capitalize on the people principle:

- Spend time with the people who need you
- Listen with intensity and an open mind
- Write positive notes to students, staff, and parents, and make other positive contacts via email, text, or phone
- Adjust your schedule so you can be fully present in classrooms and not bogged down in your office with the mundane
- Surprise your team with treats, fun adventures, and other things that will make them feel valued, appreciated, and loved
- Be vulnerable as a leader, and admit your failures and mistakes along the way
- Spread glitter everywhere, and be sure to dance a ton!
- Try new things, and be willing to change your mind
- Create a school theme you can revisit throughout the year to help deepen connections
- Be available when your team needs you . . . whenever they need you
- Never shy away from difficult decisions when you know you're doing what's best for students
- Work hard, play together, and don't take yourself too seriously

All too often as principals, we allow ourselves to get caught up in all the admin "stuff," and we miss huge opportunities to connect with the people around us and to keep them at the center of our work. Don't let that happen. You'll never regret the moments you sat in the kindergarten circle at story time, the wall-ball game you played at recess, the powerful phone call you made instead of refreshing your inbox, the dinner you shared with a teacher, or the community event you attended. Keep the people principle at the heart of all you do, and do it with every ounce of intensity and authenticity you possess as a leader.

Curt Rees (@CurtRees) is principal of State Road Elementary School in La Crosse, Wisconsin. He is also a PhD candidate in the Education Leadership Studies program at the University of Kentucky. His research interest is student data privacy. As principal, Curt models the importance of establishing relationships with students and staff. He also works intentionally to connect with all parents at the school:

> As an elementary school principal, I know how important it is for educators to build relationships with parents. Developing a partnership with parents when their children are in their first years at school will pay huge dividends over the years the kids will be attending. School principals can play a key role in this relationship building, and it isn't difficult to do.
>
> I like to focus on the time when we see the most parents at school: arrival and dismissal times. Each morning I go to the car lane at the front of school and greet kids and parents as they walk to the doors or drop kids off along the sidewalk. Most of the time, the interactions with parents are brief. They consist of a greeting, maybe a comment about the weather, or I might answer a quick question parents have about an event.
>
> Once a majority of the kids have entered the school, I'll go inside the building and do a lap through each hallway. While most of the parents say goodbye at the curb or front door, we have a few parents that like to walk their children to the classroom door. This is a great time for parents to have a face-to-face connection with their teachers, and often these interactions are about the kids who need more support. Once in a while, I'll see the child who is being emotional and is not yet ready to say goodbye to Mom or Dad. This is an opportunity to check in with them and see how I can help. Usually all that is needed is a little reassurance from me to the child (or the parent) that it's going to be a good day, and the parent will be back at the end of the day to hear all about the good stuff that will have happened.

Something that is important to me is to learn the names of the parents I see frequently during the arrival and dismissal times. I have known some of the parents for years, so those interactions are easy, as we have a history of common experiences. For new parents, I make it a point to introduce myself and welcome them to our school. During subsequent times I see them, I make it a point to use their name when I greet them. "Hi, Melissa" feels a lot more genuine than "Hi there." I don't have a sensational memory for facial recognition and name recall, so I frequently get help from the other staff around me. As I walk to the door and see a parent whose name I can't quite remember, I'll subtly check with our building secretary to look it up quickly in our student information system.

I enjoy these interactive times of the day for my own social enjoyment, but I know it also makes me more available to help parents. It's a lot more comfortable and convenient for parents to connect with me when I am in the hallway or at the front of the school than it is if I am in my office. A two-minute conversation in the hall can provide great help to a parent or at least allow us to find another time and place to talk to figure out the issue at hand.

2

PEOPLE PRINCIPLE RESOURCES

For a list of these and other resources, please visit theprincipledprincipal.com.

"Brené Brown on Empathy"
A short, animated video featuring the wisdom of Brené Brown on the topic of empathy. She shares four qualities of empathy and explains how empathy differs from sympathy.

"It's Not about the Nail"
A very short video that provides a humorous look at the importance of actively listening and not simply trying to solve the problem. Of course, in this particular case, the problem is rather obvious!

1

PEOPLE PRINCIPLE CULTURE CRUSHER

Whenever we operate in an environment with an obvious lack of trust among teachers or between teachers and administration, we are destroying the culture at the school. We maintain that a lack of trust among the professionals in a school can adversely impact the extent to which students trust us as educators. Students, regardless of age, are very intuitive and possess an uncanny knack for discerning when things are awry among the adults with whom they interact. The more we trust each other, the more our students will feel they are in a safe environment and trust us when we ask them to take a risk, tell the truth, or push themselves beyond what they think are their limits.

When trust issues exist in a school, principled principals take immediate steps to address such issues directly, honestly, professionally, and with an unyielding resolve. Such principals value relationships and know full well that the most important word in any relationship is the word *trust*. As such, they monitor their behavior regularly to ensure their words and actions foster—rather than inhibit—trust within the schoolhouse.

One model for such trustworthy behavior is the "Top 10 Trust Traits" model described by Whitaker and Zoul:

1. Be there.
2. Show you care.
3. Provide resources.
4. Communicate regularly.
5. Involve others.
6. Celebrate success.
7. Value diversity and dissent.
8. Support innovation.
9. Address underperformance.
10. Demonstrate personal integrity.

Regardless of what method is employed, our very best principals work intentionally to establish and maintain trust among all adults working in the school as one important way to shape the school's culture into one that staff, parents, and students recognize as safe and caring.

PRINCIPLE 3
The Self-Leadership Principle

The most difficult part of leadership is leading yourself.
If you can't lead yourself well,
how can you lead others?

—Nathan Eland

You are the most important person you lead. "The Leader in Me" philosophy is a school change process that does for a school the same thing an operating system does for a computer. Based on Stephen Covey's *7 Habits of Highly Effective People*, it guides the school culture and decisions and even informs the outlook and approach of the school toward parents, each other, and—most importantly—students. Becoming a "Leader in Me" school is a significant commitment and undertaking for any school, but its benefits are numerous. When schools adopt this process, all staff members participate in the *7 Habits of Highly Effective People* signature training program in preparation for "The Leader in Me" implementation.

This training is significantly different from what we are accustomed to in schools. The majority of professional learning for teachers and for ourselves focuses almost solely on students, policies, teaching strategies, and so on. It seems professional learning opportunities in schools that are focused on the development of an individual as a person are extremely rare. However, the 7 Habits training does just that, with the idea that in order for staff members to teach the 7 Habits to students, they first need to know and live the habits themselves. It makes perfect sense, but too often we do not heed this lesson.

While participating in The Leader in Me training, it isn't uncommon for principals to have an epiphany regarding how poorly they practice the habits—not only in a professional sense, but also in a personal sense. One example about which a principal told us was centered on the habit of *putting first things first*. He reflected on this idea both professionally and personally, considering how effective he was at this habit. At work, did he spend the majority of his time focused on student learning and school culture issues? Did he prioritize family time, or was he constantly checking email at the dinner table? As he pondered these questions, he found that he didn't like the answers.

We cannot successfully lead others until we successfully lead ourselves.

You may find that honestly reflecting on these habits may be disappointing to you as well. The more we discussed this experience, the more we concluded that too often in principal preparation and training, we have neglected the idea of leading ourselves. The bulk of our training has focused largely on growing, influencing, and supporting others. To be certain, influencing others is a huge part of leadership. The way we lead ourselves, however, determines how effective we will be in leading others; therefore, *you* are the most important person you lead. We cannot successfully lead others until we successfully lead ourselves. This is the basis of the self-leadership principle.

The first step to effectively leading yourself is to clarify what you stand for, both personally and professionally. It is hard to lead a school to pursue a bold vision of the future if it is not aligned with your own personal mission and vision. Simon Sinek's famous Ted Talk, *Start With Why* expertly explains that most good companies know *what* they do, but few know *why* they do it. Those companies that know why they do what they do are the most successful. The same could be said of schools. But let's take it one step further. Do you know why *you* do what you do? Why do you get out of bed every day? For whom do you do it? The answer is not simply "to be a principal." Principled principals realize they are serving a much greater purpose than merely assuming a title.

We encourage principals to make time to reflect on the three questions below, not for your school or role, but for yourself. We suggest you write these down and keep them with you. Once you have some clarity, you may wish to post them somewhere or share them with others.

What Is My Mission?

A personal mission statement is just like a school's mission statement. It is the answer to the question "Why do I exist?" Is it to be a good father or spouse? To help improve the lives of the children you serve? Asking yourself why you do what you do will help you lay a foundation that guides your work, not only as a professional but also as a person. Do not make this a school mission statement. Make it yours!

What Is My Vision?

A personal vision statement answers the question: "What do I hope to become?" If you fulfill your mission on a daily basis, eventually you should achieve your ultimate vision. So what is your vision? What do you want to become? What do you want to achieve? For what would you like to be known? Answering these questions coupled with a solid understanding of your mission or purpose will help set in motion a journey toward personal and professional excellence.

What Are My Core Values?

Core values answer the question, "How must I behave daily if I am to fulfill my mission and achieve my vision?" These core values are the ideas that should guide all our behaviors and actions, but when people think about values, it is interesting how many times they answer with what they would like to see in others. This can be valuable for inspiration, but clarifying *your* values is not about what you like in others; rather, it is about what *you* stand for. Stating, for example, that one of your core values is "honesty" means that you personally value honesty and expect it of yourself in all your relationships. The list of possible values is virtually endless. But give serious consideration to what you stand for. Is it dependability, integrity, creativity, courage, or other traits? Think of the five values that are most important to you as a person and as a leader, and write these down.

Great principals never underestimate the importance of self-leadership and constantly reflect on their growth, leadership, and learning. Leading themselves successfully helps them improve their relationships with those they lead and serve. They use these personal mission, vision, and core values to support their ongoing leadership growth as well as empowering others to lead.

Strategies for Self-Leadership

Once you have established a personal mission, vision, and core values, how do you then go about living them? Of course, there is no shortage of resources available on the topic of self-leadership. One reason the very best principals *are* the very best is because they always read and research new ideas about how to become even better. Stephen Covey, John Maxwell, and Jon Gordon are obvious names that come to mind as writers who address the subject. Others to consider include, Charles Manz, Christopher Neck, and Jeffrey Houghton. These thought leaders share strategies for maximizing self-leadership potential that we have found helpful for school leaders. In reading the works of these and other leadership experts, we tend to focus on the following strategies for success:

Set Personal and Professional Goals

Principals are no strangers to goals, whether those are related to school improvement plans, growth goals for students and teachers, or even goals for parent communication; however, great principals also work toward personal and professional goals for themselves.

What goals should you set? This is entirely up to you, of course. One personal *and* professional goal could be to complete an advanced degree. Your goal could also be to spend more time with family, possibly committing to having dinner with them at least five nights each week. It could be to unplug when you get home and put away your email and devices. It could be to run a marathon. The list of goals is endless, but great principals always seem to have two or three short-term goals they are pursuing as a way to grow and improve.

Principled principals are master modelers in all they do.

One reason setting personal goals is so vital is because this is what we ask our students to do every day. We are constantly talking to them about goals and what they want for their future selves. We preach the benefits of setting goals and achieving them. Principled principals are master modelers in all they do, including serving as examples, showing that goal setting is a lifelong process. Leaders who consistently set—and achieve—personal and professional goals are better equipped to lead and empower others.

Set Yourself Up for Success

While setting goals is important, almost equally important is setting yourself up for success in achieving those goals. It is not enough simply to have challenging personal and professional goals; you also need concrete plans for accomplishing these.

Once great principals establish what it is they want to accomplish, they set a time frame for achieving it and seek out people, opportunities, and resources that will help them stick to their plan. This often includes surrounding themselves with items that "cue" self-motivation.

Look around your office or workspace at home or at school. Are you inspired? Do you surround yourself with items that inspire and motivate you? We cannot underestimate the power of our environment. School leaders spend a great deal of time (rightly so) focusing on school culture and working to strengthen it. A school's culture is multifaceted and includes answers to three simple questions posed by any individual entering the school: 1) How does the school look? 2) How does the school feel? 3) How does the school sound? Great principals think about these three things not only for the school but also for their personal surroundings, including the principal's office.

Effective principals know what works for them in terms of accomplishing goals once they set them; for instance, one principal we know is a devout "checklist person." She usually has several checklists going at any given time. One of the first things she does every morning is take time to write a checklist for the day, keeping in mind what needs to be accomplished. Included on her checklist are personal things as well, such as exercising for thirty minutes. In her mind, it helps to be able to cross off small accomplishments one by one and then reflect at the end of the day on how, or if, she was successful. She also keeps to-do checklists for the week and month. You may find other strategies work better for you than a checklist. The important thing is to find cues and strategies that help keep you on track to achieve your short- and long-term goals.

Reward Yourself

The work we do is incredibly important. It is a privilege to do this work, but the principalship is not easy. It requires long hours, vast administrative duties, and ongoing accountability. Knowing this, great principals intentionally set aside time to reward themselves for accomplishing personal and professional goals.

A study of elementary school principals in Illinois found that rewarding oneself is an area of weakness for most school leaders. Principals reported significantly lower levels of self-reward than any other leadership category included on the survey; in fact, principals participating in the study were more than one and a half standard deviations below the mean for all other areas of personal or self-leadership. This is a statistic we need to change.

Celebrating small wins along the way will have positive benefits down the line for your entire school.

Whatever your personal and professional goals are, make sure to reward yourself when you accomplish them. It might mean taking a vacation after completing a degree or treating yourself to a nice dinner if you read ten books. The goals and the rewards themselves do not really matter; do something to celebrate *you*. When we reward ourselves for accomplishing goals, it helps support future motivation and actually accelerates goal attainment. Celebrating small wins along the way will have positive benefits down the line for your entire school. Most principals we know consider themselves servant leaders and are always on the lookout for ways to serve. This is noble, laudable, and right. Keep serving others, but do not forget to serve yourself too.

Prioritize

Tony Blair, former Prime Minister of Great Britain, stated, "The art of leadership is saying no, not yes. It is very easy to say yes." While we think schools should be places in which the principal is saying "yes" a lot, we particularly agree with Blair's point when it comes to how we manage ourselves. We all lead complex and busy lives. The difference is that some people do a better job of making clear their priorities than others. The good news is that if we are clear about our mission, vision, and core values, this road map to success has already been laid out. The challenge is making sure we stay the course.

Excellent principals are not afraid to share their personal and professional priorities with others. As principals, our professional missions included a desire to help children learn and grow so they could grow up and make the world a better place. We both saw that as being at the heart of our work as principals. At the same time, we are also personally committed to our own children and want them to be happy, successful, and productive citizens. It goes without saying that the people in our school communities appreciated the hopes and dreams we had for the students we served, but they also appreciated the fact that we had personal commitments which were equally important, commitments that tended to reflect the values of the teachers and parents in our school communities.

Take Care of Yourself

All of us have tried to start an exercise regimen, lose weight, eat healthier, or engage in some similar positive behavior. It seems so easy. Alas, like many things worth pursuing in life, it is often much easier said than done. Being a principal is the hardest job either of us has ever held; it seemed we were on the clock 24/7. Often the first thing busy principals sacrifice to "get it all done" is dedicated time to keep themselves healthy. We simply cannot underestimate the importance of staying healthy. Being a principal is a stressful job, and the harmful effects of stress are well documented. Taking care of our own physical and mental health will help us not only at work but in all other areas of our lives.

Of course, we all *want* to be healthy and exercise, but sometimes life is just so busy. Successful principals intentionally prioritize their health as something that's important to them. One principal changed his behavior after participating in the 7 Habits training we referenced earlier. For awhile, he tried to exercise when he got home from school; however, with a wife and two small kids, it always meant he was giving up time with them. The solution for him was to get up earlier in the morning to exercise before school. His kids were still in bed, and this was thirty minutes of uninterrupted personal investment. Was it hard getting up earlier? Of course. But when we prioritize things in our life—particularly our well-being—we make the time.

Personally, both of us exercise regularly, run, and can attest to the benefits we see in our work and productivity when we stick to our exercise regimen. Do not let your work take all your time and energy so there is none left to take care of yourself. Your school needs a healthy and energized principal.

Learning to Lead and Leading to Learn

One of the most important things great principals do is continue to learn. In today's world, it is vital that the principal stay up to date on the most current and innovative practices and strategies in education; in fact, we need to be the *lead learners* in our schools. There are many avenues for doing this. Of course, we can continue our formal education through graduate or professional programs, but there are other valuable ways to grow your professional knowledge that are far less expensive. Avenues such as Twitter offer educators instant access to on-demand professional development and learning. These avenues also offer a network of other professionals to call upon for advice or feedback. Some of the deepest friendships and professional relationships we have today are with other educators with whom we first connected via Twitter.

We need to be the *lead learners* in our schools.

It is also important to leverage your leadership by learning from staff members and students in your own school. Call on the people you work with on a daily basis to help you expand your knowledge. As principals, much of what we learned came from amazing teachers we observed each day.

Being What You Want Others to Be

Although there are numerous personal benefits to the self-leadership principle, there are also enormous benefits to your school and community. Being a great leader of oneself is an excellent model for others we lead, including students, staff, and parents.

As we mentioned earlier, we often talk to students about setting goals and making healthy choices. But how much more impactful is it if we are modeling those actions ourselves? As with most areas of our lives, our actions speak louder than our words. Likewise, asking our teachers to learn and try new practices can be effective, but even more effective when we lead by example. Remember, if you can't lead yourself well, how can you lead others? Start today and lead yourself to a brighter future for the well-being of yourself—and your school.

The Self-Leadership Principle

3-2-1

3

Principals' Perspectives on the Self-Leadership Principle

Dan Butler (@danpbutler) is principal of Epworth Elementary School in the Western Dubuque Community School District in Iowa. He serves as the co-moderator of Iowa Educational Chat (#IAedchat), a weekly Twitter forum held on Sunday evenings at 8:00 CST focused on the latest trends in education. As principal, Dan is always growing and learning, continually striving to become better as a school leader. At the same time, he knows the importance of balancing his professional and personal life and finds ways to intentionally grow as a father and husband which, in turn, helps him serve more effectively as principal:

> It is no secret principals and school leaders work extremely hard to provide support, leadership, encouragement, and inspiration to those they serve on a daily basis. The demands of the principalship seem to increase with each passing year, as strong efforts are made to improve curriculum alignment, increase family and stakeholder engagement, and infuse innovative instructional practices while telling the stories of success through a wide

variety of platforms. As leaders work tirelessly to improve their settings while providing the best opportunities for teachers, support staff, families, and students, they must not forget about taking care of themselves.

Principals constantly wrestle with balancing time between family and school responsibilities. I don't know if a perfect balance will ever be found; however, successful principals must take intentional steps to invest the appropriate amount of time to family and school in order to be the best version of themselves. Whether it is exercise, reading something inspirational, expressing gratitude, spending time with family members, or whatever it is that allows leaders to unwind and recharge, it is critical to make this part of the daily routine. The challenges, stresses, and intensity of the principalship can eat you up if you let them.

Exceptional school leaders realize the importance of taking care of themselves. They understand that when they are their best, they are able to give their best to their people, schools, and communities.

Scott Schwartz (@scaschwa) is principal of Walden Elementary School in Deerfield, Illinois. He previously served as assistant principal and a seventh-grade social studies teacher at Caruso Middle School in Deerfield and is proud to serve the families, staff, and students of his community. Committed to serving all stakeholders, he is most passionate about creating a strong sense of community, maximizing capacity within his school, and encouraging innovative and engaging instruction that benefits students:

> I am fortunate to serve as a principal in a very high-achieving school district—a 2016 US Department of Education National Blue Ribbon recipient—where I am held to a high standard of professional excellence. In order to meet community expectations and in order to always do what is right for my staff and students, it

is incumbent upon me to model the way as a lifelong lead learner and to continue to grow personally and professionally every day.

To stay informed of best practices in instruction and educational leadership, I utilize tools like Twitter and Voxer. Following other educators on Twitter allows me to garner instantaneous, high-quality, and pertinent professional resources that play a relevant role in my growth and development. Likewise, Twitter chats allow me to connect with and learn from peers on a variety of specific educational topics. Voxer is a walkie-talkie app that, in the simplest form, allows me to conveniently communicate with colleagues; however, in a more fruitful manner, it allows me to connect with peers and colleagues from across the country to learn and grow.

I participate in a Voxer chat called Principals in Action in which approximately 132 principals are virtually connected and chime in daily on a variety of educational topics. The conversation flows based on participants' questions, blog posts, and inquiries. In one case, I was seeking a quality interview question to conclude a teacher interview scheduled for the following day. I posed that question to the Voxer chat group and received excellent suggestions. Other times we collaborate on ways to improve culture or increase student achievement, both of which bring about ideas I can introduce immediately. I have a great deal of respect for the principals in this Voxer group and am inspired by their collective belief that all students can learn and deserve the very best from us.

There are other areas in which I take deliberate action to learn and grow. I completed my doctoral work in 2015, I make efforts to attend and present at national, state, and local conferences, and I am frequently reading professional books that allow me to stay current. The community I serve values education and rightfully holds me to a very high standard of modeling lifelong learning. Always being mindful of ways to improve my own craft while simultaneously encouraging the incredible staff to do the same allows our school community to achieve success.

Theresa Stager (@PrincipalStager) is currently an assistant principal at Saline High School in Saline, Michigan. She is a co-host of *PrincipalPLN* podcast, which can be found at PrincipalPLN.com and on iTunes, and she is a keynote speaker and presenter at many state and national conferences. Theresa prides herself on being a servant leader and basing decisions on what is best for kids. She also knows that to lead others, she must also find ways to lead herself by growing and learning each day:

> My philosophy on leadership has always been to grow those around me to be the best they can be at whatever they aspire to. I learned a long time ago that the only way to do that is servant leadership: remembering why I'm here in the first place. In order for me to be the best I can be, I work with as many different types of leaders as I can and try to learn from all of them.
>
> Motivational speaker Jim Rohn says you are the average of the five people you spend the most time with, so I try to surround myself with the very best. Whether it's using Voxer with a practicing administrator in my Professional Learning Network (PLN) to solve a problem or Tweeting resources for a successful activity, I collaborate and communicate. Conferences are another wonderful way to learn from a large number of professional colleagues and to meet your PLN members in person. Honestly, any way you can make a true connection with another school administrator is worth the investment. You will grow yourself as a leader and, in turn, build your capacity to lead those in your own school community.

2

SELF-LEADERSHIP PRINCIPLE RESOURCES

For a list of these and other resources,
please visit theprincipledprincipal.com.

"Personal Mission Statements Of 5 Famous CEOs (And Why You Should Write One Too)"

Establishing personal mission and vision statements as well as core values are pillars of the Self-Leadership Principle. To get you started thinking about your own, here are five examples of real-life personal mission statements from leaders who rocked the world, including Richard Branson and Oprah Winfrey.

Self-Leadership: The Definitive Guide to Personal Excellence

This is a book we highly recommend for all school leaders. The book offers practical advice for leading yourself to personal excellence and is based on simple yet revolutionary principles emphasized in this chapter. The book also includes the "Revised Self-Leadership Questionnaire" (RSLQ) referenced in the study we cited in this chapter.

1

SELF-LEADERSHIP PRINCIPLE CULTURE CRUSHER

When educators lose the desire to grow as professionals, they are destroying the culture at that school. Principled principals leading exceptional schools find ways to ensure that all staff members are continuously growing, connecting, learning, leading, and improving. They do this in many ways, but one of the primary ways they encourage others to keep growing professionally is to make it known, through words and actions, that they themselves are working to improve.

The energy and enthusiasm they bring to their own learning is contagious, motivating those they serve to also keep growing. In addition, these principals learn as much as possible about each staff member they serve, including what each individual's goals, interests, passions, strengths, and learning preferences are. Armed with this knowledge, these principals design personalized professional learning opportunities. In addition to mandatory school-wide or district professional learning events, these opportunities allow each staff member to learn what they want, when they want, and how they want. Principled principals build school culture by increasing the knowledge, skills, and capabilities of each staff member at the school—starting with themselves.

PRINCIPLE 4
The Outcomes Principle

The good-to-great leaders never wanted to become larger-than-life heroes. They never aspired to be put on a pedestal or become unreachable icons. They were seemingly ordinary people quietly producing extraordinary results.

—Jim Collins

If any researcher has identified what great leaders do to produce extraordinary results, that researcher, in our opinion, is Jim Collins. Collins's book *Good to Great* is a staple in both education and business arenas for good reason.

The real nuggets of wisdom that Collins uncovers are not so much about the companies studied but the leaders of those companies. Collins describes different levels of leaders, with the highest being the "Level 5" leader. Level 5 leaders possess a combination of personal humility and professional will. Personal humility means the leader is not worried about who gets the credit. The work and results are the reward for a job well done. Professional will, meanwhile, is about an intense focus on outcomes and results. These leaders are pushed to success by the clarity of their focus. Level 5 leaders help businesses get better, in part, by focusing on outcomes. Serving as a Level 5 leader is also at the heart of the outcomes principle for school leaders. Every school in the United States needs a level 5 leader as principal to ensure we have great—rather than merely "good"—schools.

What Is an Outcome?

What is an outcome? How is it different from a goal? An outcome is defined by Webster as "something that follows as a result or consequence." The keywords in this definition are *something that follows.* Setting improvement goals in schools has become a commonplace occurrence, and that's a good thing. We meet in Professional Learning Communities (PLCs) or as a school leadership team to establish goals. Maybe the goal is to improve reading or vocabulary skills, or perhaps it focuses on addition or multiplication. We have become skilled at creating goals, but it is not enough to simply *have* goals. Great principals know how to translate goals into actions and, ultimately, into results. When a school doesn't meet a goal, we sometimes decide it was too lofty a goal and dismiss it with a "you win some; you lose some" mentality. But if we properly translate goals into actions and focus on outcomes, failure should be a very rare and disconcerting result.

Great principals know how to translate goals into actions and, ultimately, into results.

One principal we know was disappointed in her school's progress in math. The students at this school were lagging behind similar schools not only in the district but compared to schools in surrounding communities. It was clear to the principal that the focus of the new school year would be improving math performance. The principal rallied teachers, met with them in teams, showed them the trend data, and insisted that each grade level create goals that focused on improvement in math.

The teachers complied with the request and created goals stating students in their grade levels would improve in math. The principal moved on to other initiatives. Fast forward through winter and into spring, and students at this school had not measurably improved in math performance.

Frustrated, the principal discussed the results with teachers, and all the normal refrains were voiced. Some said it was the students. "You know our kids are different than kids in other schools," they said, even though the comparative schools and communities were nearly identical. Some said, even though the results were poor, they still felt like they accomplished the goal because they felt "kids like math more." Still others were convinced they were making improvements and did not understand why the data did not show it. In the end, most teachers came up with excuses, even though they were clearly falling short of their stated goals. The principal agreed they had done some good work and complimented the teams on their efforts.

The adults found reasons to feel good about their work while their students still lagged in math performance.

This is a good example of a well-intentioned principal falling short. It is perfectly appropriate to create goals for students, whether academic or social-emotional; however, the principal in this case thought that merely establishing motivating goals would be enough. Many teachers walked away, goal in hand, and went back to their classrooms to do the same things they had always done.

Lofty goals must be accompanied by intentional actions. Schools that successfully turn goals into actions focus not on the goal, but on the *outcome* associated with the goal. The difference between a vague goal and a specific outcome is scope. A vague goal has a broad focus such as "We will improve third-grade math scores." Specific outcomes take such statements quite a bit further, drilling down to specific skills. Of course, ensuring vague goals are rewritten into Specific, Measurable, Attainable, Results-oriented, and Time-bound (SMART) goals helps to focus on outcomes. But again, the overall purpose of writing goals, even SMART goals, is to ensure we are attaining the results we need to attain. These outcomes must be associated with some measurement tool—whether large scale, such as focusing on improving scores on the state assessment, or smaller scale, such as grade-level or departmental common assessments. SMART goals must include outcomes which, in turn, must be based on measurable indicators. Focusing on such outcomes naturally begs the appropriate question: How do we get there?

Schools led by principled principals are intensely focused on outcomes at all times. These are also schools in which kids and teachers are having fun, teaching and learning practices are innovative, and students are engaged as meaning-makers as opposed to mere meaning-seekers. Educators in such schools measure, evaluate, and monitor their actions and related results every step of the way. In addition, principals hold themselves accountable for outcomes and hold others accountable as well. When we don't achieve an outcome or meet a goal, we should not find reasons to feel good about this. We should acknowledge the efforts made, but we must also confront the brutal facts that our goals were not met and begin again, with fierce intention, to do what we must to achieve our goals.

Data Driven or Student Driven?

We often hear terms such as "data driven" or "data informed" to describe the practices of schools, principals, and teachers when analyzing student performance. Many educators have moved from using the term "data driven" to "data informed" when discussing outcomes. Data informed suggests using student data as just one piece of the puzzle, knowing there are numerous other variables associated with student learning that can impact performance. We also hear the term "evidence driven," suggesting educators should look at multiple measures, or pieces of evidence, relating to outcomes; for instance, would a student need to write an essay if they chose to demonstrate their learning with a video? Finally, we hear the term "student driven" being bandied about, which seems to suggest a combination of all the above in which data points and evidence are just pieces of the puzzle. We wonder if there is really a difference among these terms employed to describe actions and student achievement—or if these differences are merely semantic? Although we understand the subtle distinctions among them, our contention is that data driven is data informed is evidence driven is student driven.

The first belief we must adopt is that our schools exist for the purpose of student learning.

Being a data-driven school means being a student-driven school, yet the first belief we must adopt as part of our mission as educators is that our schools exist for the purpose of student learning. That's it, the whole ball game: student learning. All our goals are accomplished by accepting this single vital truth.

To understand the results of our efforts, we need rigorous assessments. Unfortunately, educators have become part of the problem here. We have railed against state assessments and accountability as loudly as any other group, including parents and politicians. Successful schools, however, where students are learning at high levels, know that state assessments like PARCC, ACT, and SAT are not the enemy; instead, the enemy of student learning is complacency and a lack of accountability. Great principals focus their schools on intentional and innovative teaching and learning practices so students succeed regardless of the assessment.

We know a principal who has achieved tremendous success with this philosophy. During the 2014–2015 school year, there was a contentious nationwide rally against new state-mandated assessments such as the Partnership for Assessment of Readiness for College and Careers (PARCC) and Smarter Balanced assessments. Resistance came not only from many parents and politicians but also educators themselves. The northern Chicago suburbs, where we served as administrators, were not immune to this revolt. Some of the surrounding school districts had their own superintendents sending letters of protest to state officials about the assessment. Other districts seemed to encourage parents to direct their children to refuse the test or keep them out of school altogether.

In the midst of all the furor, this particular principal and his entire staff and parent community remained relatively unaffected by the uproar and, instead, simply focused on what they did every single day: providing rigorous, engaging, relevant learning experiences designed to yield high levels of student learning. After the assessment results came out for the 2014-2015 school year, the school had performed as well as any school in the entire state. When asked about the exemplary scores by a reporter from a major newspaper, this principal's reply was simple: "We really didn't make a huge deal about it."

Since the 2014–2015 school year, this school's student achievement scores on PARCC and every other measure have continued to increase. Each year the school is ranked among the top schools in the state. This is a public school in a middle-class community in the northern suburbs. It is not in the poorest community in the state by any measurement, but it is certainly not the most affluent, either. Compared to other schools around the United States, it is more alike than different in every way except one: superior student achievement.

It's not about the assessment; it's about the learning.

What is their secret? Again, this principal summed it up quite succinctly: "We really didn't make a huge deal about it."

If we lead our schools with the mindset that our students will be successful regardless of what test or assessment we put in front of them, they will be successful. Ask students to write an essay? No problem. Make a video or multimedia presentation? Thought you'd never ask! Solve real-world math problems and write a narrative about your process? Piece of cake. It's not about the assessment; it's about the learning. If we are teaching kids at high levels with rigorous standards and putting them in charge of their learning, they will be successful at anything. It is largely a myth that the assessment is the problem. Students who are prepared for twenty-first-century learning expectations through daily twenty-first-century learning experiences designed by twenty-first-century educators who do not fret about standards can knock any assessment out of the park.

This is an example of a student-driven school. All students learn at high levels and achieve rigorous standards, and this is made possible by intentionally focusing on all available data. Teachers focus on where students are on a variety of measures and focus on what is needed to move them to the next level. A student in fourth grade who is ready for fifth-grade math does fifth-grade math. Students are not held back or pushed too far beyond their next personal best. Data is used to clearly identify where students are and what subsequent actions must be taken. If principals, teachers, and students are focused on the right work, successful outcomes will almost always follow.

Data driven is student driven. Principals who are masters of the outcomes principle do not quibble about semantics surrounding this topic. They also do not complain about measures and what they mean. They lead teachers and lead students to learning levels that go far *beyond* state and national assessments.

Death by Binder

There is perhaps nothing that signifies the problems and pitfalls of improving schools more than the three-ring binder. Walk into any principal's office and you will likely see this staple of hindered progress somewhere on a shelf.

These items were not intended to be the fantastic dust collectors they are. At one time, teams of administrators and teachers got together and painstakingly worked to create these beautiful and intricate plans. They became "official" by being placed into a three-ring binder. Then they were carefully transferred to a shelf, and that is where they usually stayed. We wonder how many school improvement plans have made their way to a principal's bookshelf to live out their days?

There is no more dreaded symbol of stagnation in the world of school administration than the school improvement plan in a three-ring binder. But it doesn't have to be this way. Schools need not live and die by the plan in the binder—not if we're focused on outcomes. Don't get us wrong: It is very important to have plans for improving our schools. We may even put these in binders. The binder itself is not the problem. When a principal helps teachers focus on results, these plans are actually reviewed and revised to help them achieve future performance goals. The best principals we know are focused on outcomes and have their plans marked up for continual improvement. These documents can be valued as living, breathing resources for principals and teachers.

School plans must include a laser-like specificity about what will be done for certain groups of students as well as individual students.

The secret to creating real school improvement plans is to begin with outcomes and then work our way back. Our plans also need to contain those things we *will* do, not things we *should* do. There should be absolute clarity in the school not only about what goals we have but also what outcomes we expect when those goals are achieved. This is the key to a new kind of plan that will drive real change. Many school plans look only at a grade level of students as a whole. This is too large a group to truly impact with one or two strategies. School plans must include a laser-like specificity about what will be done for certain groups of students as well as individual students.

Consider a very common example: In most states, there is a method for reporting the percentage of students in a school, and grade levels within that school, who are meeting state expectations. In Illinois, for example, schools administer the state assessment (PARCC) to all students in grades 3–8. A K–5 school with an enrollment of six hundred students would have approximately one hundred students at each grade level. That means in a K–5 school, one hundred students would be tested in each grade. If you have one hundred students in any one grade level, then each student represents about 1 percent of the total percentage of students meeting grade-level expectations; for example, if third grade has one hundred students and 60 percent meet state expectations and 40 percent do not, then sixty students met expectations while forty students did not. If we want to improve the percentage of students who meet grade-level expectations, we must be specific about what individual students need.

We should continue to provide rigorous expectations for *all* our students; however, we must also address the students who are not on track for college readiness. If, over the course of the school year, we can specifically identify the learning needs of actual students, helping ten more meet expectations, we will have moved that grade level from 60 percent meeting expectations to 70 percent. If we can get twenty students there, we will go from 60 percent to 80 percent. The goal, obviously, is for 100 percent of students to meet grade-level expectations, and principals dedicated to the outcomes principle are never satisfied when even one student is not performing at or above grade-level standards. Rather than focusing on the percentages, they focus on something much more important: real, individual kids, with real learning needs, who need real learning plans. Looking at each individual child is how they make a difference and, ultimately, realize large-scale improvements in student learning.

Measure by Measure

In today's schools, most principals are equipped with an enormous amount of data pertaining to academic performance. But what about data relating to other important areas critical to school success, such as school culture and student engagement? These are variables that make student academic achievement possible. Management guru Peter Drucker maintained, "If you can't measure it, you can't manage it." We would add that you can't improve it, either. This is why great principals measure much more than student learning. They measure *everything* that matters.

> ## Great principals measure much more than student learning. They measure *everything* that matters.

Does your school have a positive, productive culture? How do you know? Culture is about how the school collectively behaves and operates, including the way it feels, looks, and sounds. Believe it or not, there are ways to quantify these attributes.

There is no shortage of school culture surveys available. For the past four years, Deerfield Public Schools District 109 in Illinois has utilized the INSIGHTeX school culture survey from Humanex Ventures to gather and analyze school culture data. This survey consists of eighty-eight statements that measure fifteen different dimensions of school culture. These dimensions include pride, innovation, engagement, satisfaction, and relationships. Every staff member at every school participates in this survey annually, and school teams analyze the data to identify areas of strength as well as areas for improvement.

Principals in Deerfield Public Schools take this information, share results openly with all staff members at the school, and create plans to improve the culture. Often, school teams focus on the five to ten survey statements on which they scored the lowest and identify root causes as well as possible solutions. One survey question that arose as a "bottom five" item at one principal's school related to staff members receiving opportunities for coaching from the principal to improve their professional practice. As a result, this principal worked with her team and set a goal to meet with every staff member at least once throughout the course of the year, taking them through a structured coaching conversation. The conversation centered completely on the staff member: What kind of professional development opportunities would they like? What did they want to learn? And most importantly, how could the principal help them?

The results were noticeable. On the next year's culture survey, responses to that statement increased significantly. More importantly, a school principal was now actively involved in helping teachers and other staff members grow as professionals.

Many principals talk about school culture and make attempts to improve it, but without concrete data and plans, we are merely dancing in the dark. Some actions we take may work, but it will largely be a matter of chance whether these are the right areas of focus. The principal in our example systematically improved her school culture by making concrete plans, bringing staff members into the process, and monitoring progress.

This school district also measures student engagement. Students in grades three through eight take a student engagement survey annually that measures how engaged they are in their own learning. The survey includes questions about their teachers, how students best learn, and the amount of choices they have in their learning. The results of the first survey were revealing. Students across the district do quite well academically when compared to schools around the state. While the statewide average percentage of students meeting or exceeding grade-level standards is approximately 30 percent, Deerfield's is closer to 80 percent. When the district administered its first student engagement survey, however, they were surprised to find that some results were less than stellar; for example, the lowest area of engagement according to student responses was in the area of student choice. Students reported they had very little choice in their learning and believed what they were learning was not meaningful. Even though these students were academically successful, a significant majority of them felt what they were learning was not relevant to their future and that they had little choice in how they learned.

This information led to significant changes at all schools in the district. These changes were initiated not only by principals and teachers but by students as well. Again, the data was shared publicly with staff and students, and each group brainstormed ways to improve. Several schools developed concrete plans for how students could choose activities to work on in the classroom. Some schools even organized weekly and monthly student Edcamps, where students could choose the topics about which to research and learn. Some schools did cross-grade exploration. At one school, second-grade students brainstormed a list of topics about which they wanted to learn more. They were then organized into groups based on their top choices, then fifth-grade students designed lessons and led the learning for their younger peers for an entire afternoon.

When these schools started actually listening to their students and looking into the data on student engagement, the path to improvement became clear. This experience was yet another reminder that school leaders should not just measure student academic learning, but all aspects of the school experience, especially school culture and student engagement.

This is something any principal can get started on right now. They can create their own survey, partner with a company such as Humanex Ventures as was done in Deerfield (for additional information, please see the resource link at the end of this chapter), or simply conduct a quick Google search for culture surveys and student surveys.

We cannot improve what we do not measure. The outcomes principle is about identifying our current reality and then using all available data to problem solve and improve.

When Data Speaks, Do We Listen?

One of the commitments Anthony made this past year was to eat healthier. To do this, he downloaded an app to track everything he ate. The app provided detailed information, including calories, cholesterol, added sugars, and carbohydrates consumed each day. This proved to be an incredibly powerful tool and a great example of how today's technology gives us access to information that was previously unavailable.

It also makes interpreting and analyzing the information simpler than ever before.

However, when he began tracking the data and realized he may have been eating too many carbohydrates or added sugars, the real action needed to happen. He had to change eating habits to improve those numbers. Among other things, this meant choosing frozen yogurt rather than ice cream and cutting way back on his doughnut intake. Easier said than done!

Our point is that data is ubiquitous in society today, both in our schools and in our lives outside of school. All schools can collect and analyze almost endless types of data. Once we commit to this, we must also commit to accepting it at face value, listening to what the numbers are telling us, and acting accordingly.

There is no logical excuse not to "like the data." We may not like what it is telling us, but our response must be to do something about it rather than find fault with the data or pretend it does not exist. The data is there to help us. We have known principals who selectively "cherry pick" data and tweak certain items so their school performance looks a bit better than what an objective view of all the data would suggest.

We have also heard principals say things like, "Well, even though the data is not where it should be, we know what we are doing is great for kids." No, we don't. This is one of the worst things a school leader can say. If our measures are valid and reliable, data reveals the truth. We have to make the human choice to listen to it and make changes.

The principled principal always views data from an objective standpoint and does not let it reflect on them or their teachers personally. These principals assign no blame or fault, but they also accept no excuses. They treat data as a friend that helps them make improvements.

The Outcomes Principle
3–2–1

3

PRINCIPALS' PERSPECTIVES ON THE OUTCOMES PRINCIPLE

Kristin Harper (@TXCoolPrinc) is principal of James Randolph Elementary School in Katy ISD, located in Texas, near Houston. She has led numerous professional development sessions on Balanced Literacy and has implemented the components of a Professional Learning Community on her campus to include flexible scheduling, embedded professional development, collaboration, common assessments, and data analysis. Here, Kristin shares how she and her team ensure each student at the school is prepared for the next step in their individual journeys:

> I recently saw a phrase on social media that stated, "Teachers aren't in it for the income, they are in it for the outcome." What an honor and privilege it is to be a part of a profession in which the outcome is better lives for our children. I opened our school as the principal three years ago, and we began talking about what kind of school we wanted for the community we serve. We had many discussions about ensuring each student was prepared for the next step in his or her journey.
>
> What does "prepared" mean? We, of course, want our students to be prepared academically, meaning we want them to achieve at high levels, to be critical thinkers and problem solvers,

and to consistently meet or exceed expected progress. In order to achieve this, we know we must focus on instruction first and consistently measure the effectiveness of our instructional practices through ongoing formative assessments. As a result, we built time into our schedule for teachers to collaboratively develop common assessments at the beginning of each teaching unit in order to track student progress toward learning goals. Teachers regularly meet with our instructional coaches and administrators to review student data on both individual student performance and overall grade-level performance on specific objectives. As the leader of the campus, it is my responsibility to ensure there is time devoted to disaggregating student data in order to ensure students are learning and to assist teachers in developing a plan for intervention for those students who experience difficulty.

Let me be clear that we believe the state assessment is important; however, it is not the only measure we should use to determine student success. We make this point clear with our staff, students, and community. The state standardized test is one instrument that is used to measure success, but by no means does it encompass all that the child knows and can do.

Another outcome we want for our students is to be prepared socially and interpersonally. We make it a focus on our campus to make sure our children have many opportunities to engage with each other through collaboration, creativity, communication, and real-world problem solving. We have a rapidly growing student population as we are in a community that is one of the fastest growing in the state of Texas. When we opened in 2014, we had 750 students, and three years later, we have a projected enrollment of 1360. As a result, we put specific procedures and practices in place to ensure student dialogue and group collaboration. We also know that, in order for our students to be prepared for careers in the future, they must have not only knowledge and skills pertaining to the occupation but also skills in collaboration, communication, creativity, and problem solving.

In order to foster this climate, we encourage teachers to make time for community circles each day in which students learn communication skills as well as conflict resolution. Our instructional coaches work with our teachers to ensure instructional strategies include time for collaborative projects and group discussions such as "accountable talk" in reading. We have also implemented a school-wide enrichment model in which students are able to explore something they are passionate about or interested in with students who have the same interests.

At the end of last school year, I brought together a group of our out-going fifth-grade students to ask specific questions about their experiences at our school. They shared their love for the climate and environment we had established through opportunities to interact with their peers, and they emphasized that their favorite teachers were ones who cared about them but, at the same time, had high expectations for them. These are the outcomes we should all strive for as educators.

Danny Steele (@SteeleThoughts) is an award-winning principal from Birmingham, Alabama. He is passionate about connecting with kids, inspiring teachers, and building positive school culture. He writes an education leadership blog (steelethoughts.com) that has received over two million page views. Danny knows results matter and works intentionally with staff members to ensure the school is reaching its goals:

At Thompson Sixth-Grade Center, we don't want to get better by accident; we want to get better on purpose. Data is what allows us to be strategic in our school improvement efforts. The data wall in the main hallway of our school showcases the data from our previous standardized test results along with the progress of our benchmark scores during the current school year. It serves as a point of pride for how far we've come and as a motivator for how far we still need to go. Additionally, every summer our leadership team has the opportunity to analyze survey data from all our stakeholder groups. In these surveys, we can gather information on whether our parents think our school's purpose statement is focused on students' success, or if our teachers believe the administration fosters a culture of collaboration and innovation, and whether our students feel adequately prepared for the next grade.

The school improvement process is too important to have goals that are arbitrary or merely based on anecdotes. We want to use student achievement data to refine our instructional program, and we want to use survey data to strengthen our school's culture. When teachers and school leaders take the time to understand their own data, it creates a sense of urgency to rise above the status quo. It compels us to want more, to do more, and to be more for our students. They deserve it. We are driven by data because we are inspired by kids.

Jeff Mann (@Mann4edu) is principal of A&M Consolidated Middle School in College Station ISD, College Station, Texas. In his seven years of public school administration experience, Jeff has worked as a high school assistant principal and an intermediate school and middle school principal. Jeff has been recognized by Texas A&M University's Department of Education as a transformational leader in 2017 and has been a member of the Texas Principal's Vision Institute since 2014. Jeff knows outcomes matter and shares three specific outcomes he promotes and monitors in his school community:

> As the campus principal, I have a responsibility to know that my campus is achieving success. Measuring outcomes is critical to determining the success or shortcomings of my campus. Of course, there are the obvious outcomes related to state assessments, but I am not as interested in those outcomes because of the high-stress, high-stakes, and unrealistic nature of those assessments. I prefer to measure outcomes related to classroom formative assessments,

intervention strategies, and instructional coaching. Each of these outcomes is critical to the success of my school because they look at different aspects of teaching and learning. Let's examine each one a little closer as they relate to outcomes.

Classroom formative assessment allows us to gather real time feedback, as well as provide our students feedback as quickly as possible. I encourage and support my teachers in utilizing technology as a part of the formative assessment process. Formative assessment technology allows teachers to gather data quickly, assess the data, provide feedback to students, and reshape teaching in real time. The formative assessment process improves the learning outcomes because students are able to receive feedback that improves their learning.

Intervention strategies are utilized frequently to support struggling learners, but we must ensure that our interventions are successful. When I measure outcomes related to interventions, I examine data collected by the math and reading specialists and classroom grades once interventions begin. I also host classroom teachers' conferences with struggling students to ask them how they feel they are doing in a class with the interventions. Measuring the outcomes of student learning during and after interventions help us to determine if the intervention is effective and should be continued.

Perhaps one of the most effective ways to influence the learning outcomes of a school is through instructional coaching. All great athletes have coaches telling them what they need to do to improve their performance. Excellent athletic coaches provide specific feedback time and time again to their athletes with a variety of tools and communication approaches. We should be doing the same for our teachers. Coaching is not something we do to teachers; it is done with teachers. Specific feedback is provided in coaching conversations. Observation notes and videos are reviewed together, and next steps are developed and agreed upon as a pair. This approach to instructional coaching allows the teacher to have ownership in the process which leads to the implementation of changes in the classroom. As a result, the changes to instructional practices lead to outcomes in student performance that show student learning is improving.

When I measure the outcomes of classroom formative assessments, intervention strategies, and instructional coaching, the outcomes of state assessments take care of themselves. By focusing on high levels of teaching and learning in our schools, we push our students to the level of excellence they deserve. When we focus on excellence, the outcomes take care of themselves.

2

Outcomes Principle Resources

For a list of these and other resources, please visit theprincipledprincipal.com.

"Creating SMART Goals"

This short video clip features Professional Learning Communities leader Rebecca DuFour explaining SMART goals, including short-term goals and "stretch goals." Note that when she talks about the "R" in "SMART," she emphasizes the fact that "we are all about student-learning results" in schools.

INSIGHTeX Snapshot℠ *(principles.humanexventures.com)*

This is a quick survey that will give you an introduction to measuring your school's culture. It is an abbreviated version of the full survey we reference in this chapter.

1

OUTCOMES PRINCIPLE
CULTURE CRUSHER

When school leaders use data to punish instead of using data to ask questions, problem solve, and improve, we destroy the culture of the school. As important as we think outcomes and results are, we cannot "punish" kids or teachers when they do not meet expectations. At the same time, we cannot lie or pretend the results are meaningless. Our kids deserve to know where they stand in terms of their performance compared to grade-level standards. Our teachers also deserve to know whether their results show that the students they teach are meeting growth targets.

When results are positive, we should recognize and celebrate this with students and staff. At times, of course, some students and some teachers will fall short of where they need to be. How we respond in such instances is even more important than our responses when results are favorable. Our response must be honest but supportive. There must be no adverse consequences for a student who does not meet academic goals or for a teacher whose students perform poorly. We have known school leaders who withhold special classes, events, or recess for students who are struggling academically. This is not the answer; these students need those opportunities as much or more than students who are thriving academically. Teachers, too, must not be "punished" when some students they teach do not meet standards.

In both cases, however, it is important that we act. High levels of student learning are non-negotiable, but we must act to support, not to punish. We must go back to the data, "hear" what it is telling us, talk to students and teachers who may be struggling, hear what they are telling us, and then design individual plans for students and teachers who need our support. Principled principals use data to build the culture, not destroy it.

PRINCIPLE 5
The Talent Principle

Hire character. Train skill.

—Peter Schutz

Great teachers can change the trajectory of a child's life. They can help students learn and grow at high levels and inspire them to have bold dreams for their future. Such teachers can also positively impact their colleagues and the overall school culture.

On the other hand, poor teachers can hinder student growth. They can also be poisonous to a school's culture and incite infighting, gossip, and distrust among the staff. One of the most important things we do in schools is hire new staff members. When we get it right and hire great people, our schools improve overnight; however, when we make a mistake in this area, it can negatively impact students, staff, and the school culture for years, possibly decades. Hiring new staff members is ridiculously important. Unfortunately, it is also something that many schools do haphazardly and arbitrarily.

Consider these two questions: 1) How long does it take to realize we have made a bad hiring decision? 2) How long does it take for that person to leave?

Chances are, the answer to the first question is "Not very long." Most principals can decide pretty quickly into the school year whether they have made a wise hiring decision. It could be as short as a week but probably not longer than a month. The second question is a bit more complicated, possibly depending on state and local district policies. At a minimum, however, the school will be stuck with that teacher for the remainder of the school year. Worse yet, students will probably be stuck with him or her as well. Our schools and our children simply cannot afford hiring mistakes.

Principled principals do everything in their power to surround themselves with talented people.

Of course, we can take all kinds of action steps to improve teacher performance, and we should. Just because some-one has poor practice today doesn't mean they always will. And even the very best teachers we hire will need (and want) ongoing support to continuously improve. But it's much eas-ier to hire the right people from the outset—people who are both highly qualified and highly effective, people hardwired to improve with ongoing training. We would much rather invest additional time, energy, and effort on the front end of the hiring process to ensure we are making an excellent hiring decision than to spend inordinate amounts of time after the fact trying to rehabilitate a less-than-stellar educator. Principled principals do everything in their power to surround themselves with talented people.

Hiring the Right People

Shortly after Anthony graduated from college, he moved to Chicago. Only twenty-three years of age, he wasn't 100 percent sure about his career path. One day he wandered into the Four Seasons Hotel in downtown Chicago and applied for a job as a server in the restaurant. A friend had told him the money was good and the hours were flexible, so he gave it a try.

If you are familiar with the Four Seasons Hotels and Resorts, you know these are five-star establishments with the highest standards of luxury and service. Anthony assumed that working as a server for the Four Seasons would be no big deal. As a poor college student, he had waited tables in various establishments. Of course, these places had names like "The Tumbleweed." Working at The Four Seasons was a far cry from serving at restaurants in western Kentucky.

Much to his surprise, he had to go through *five* interviews to eventually get the job waiting tables. First, he met with the human resources director, then the manager of the lounge and restaurant, then the Assistant Director of Food and Beverage, then the Director of Food and Beverage, and, finally, the general manager of the hotel. Sitting in the plush office of the general manager overlooking Michigan Avenue, he was finally offered a job.

Working at Four Seasons proved to be a great job. Fellow employees were fantastic, among the nicest and friendliest people with whom Anthony had ever worked. If he ever needed help, there was always someone ready and willing to lend a hand. The managers were professional and friendly, always reducing stress levels associated with the job and helping out wherever needed. The place ran like a well-oiled machine. And this was no accident.

After about three months of working there, the general manager came in for breakfast and Anthony waited on him. He asked this manager a question that had been on his mind: "Why did you hire me?" The gentleman looked surprised, so Anthony explained that he had no experience in hotels, no experience with fine dining or the service industry, and he was sure a lot of people had applied for the job, considering the five interviews. Many of those other applicants for the job had probably worked at some of the finest establishments in the city; instead, he hired a twenty-three-year-old, right out of school, with zero experience and a southern twang.

The manager smiled as if he were holding a secret and then said, "We hire people." He went on to explain how experience, education, and training can be valuable but tell you nothing about a person's character. The character of the people you hire is the key factor.

The character of the people you hire is the key factor.

That day Anthony realized why the Four Seasons was so successful. They had a hiring system that was about identifying one thing: character. The manager explained that any person can be taught a skill; what cannot be taught is how to smile when things don't go right, how to be a good coworker, and how to care about what you are doing. "These things," he said, "comprise one's character, who they are, and that is what we look for when we hire." The Four Seasons Hotels and Resorts have become the gold standard in their industry, and the secret to their success revolves around one thing: hiring the right people.

So, how do we get the right people to serve in our schools? Some districts with multiple schools may have a process for hiring people involving many principals because over the years, teachers move from one school to another. All the more reason to hire a person with the human qualities you seek. These people will be able to adapt and flow with new challenges as they may move from school to school. In some districts, the principal has input but not the final decision regarding whom to recommend to the Board for a teaching position. We hope this is the exception rather than the rule and suggest that if you are in that situation, you work to change the process.

Principals are responsible for all aspects of their school, and success is wholly dependent on those with whom they surround themselves. If principals cannot select their team members when openings arise, they are already at a disadvantage in building a positive culture.

What Should We Value?

Assuming we agree about the importance of hiring only great people in our schools, the natural question then becomes "What should we value when hiring new staff?" What should we look for in a great teacher, nurse, or any other school hire? Many district and school leaders place an exceedingly high value on experience and education. While these can be valuable in hiring and should not be ignored, are they the most important indicators of a good hire? Let's consider the way great principals look at each of these areas.

Experience

Whenever we speak to parents or those outside of the education profession, they always seem stunned when they learn research does not support the idea that class size matters in regard to student learning; in fact, we bet that if we asked families at almost any school around the country one thing we could do to improve student learning, they might well say, "Reduce class size." On the surface, this seems like a completely reasonable idea: The fewer students in a classroom, the more direct attention they should receive from the teacher. Hence, the thinking goes, the more they would learn.

Let's put aside for a moment the idea that learning from other students and small-group work are also ways to learn and don't involve one-to-one contact with the teacher. We know there are excellent ways to structure high-level learning in classrooms with higher numbers of students where learning occurs in numerous ways, with direct instruction from the classroom teacher being just one example; instead, let's focus on why class size does not matter in terms of student learning. The primary differentiator is the quality of the teacher.

When we explain this to parents, many experience a "light-bulb moment" because it makes so much sense. A poor teacher with thirty students will be a poor teacher if the class is reduced to twenty students. The lower number of students does not make their instructional methods any more effective. A smaller class size will not increase a teacher's motivation or skill. However, a great teacher who is passionate, committed, and reflective of their practice will work wonders for twenty students and work these same wonders with thirty students. We concede it is possible for a great teacher to get more out of students with a smaller class size. But the reason class size does not bear out as a factor on student achievement in the research is because it assumes the quality of instruction is static. In reality, the quality of instruction is the true difference maker.

We think of work experience in this same way. Just because a teacher has more years of experience does not automatically mean they are a more effective teacher. We do not advocate completely ignoring previous professional experiences, but the question becomes *What experiences should we value?*

When evaluating resumes of candidates with interview teams, this point is further driven home. It always seems that some interview team members gravitate toward candidates with a great deal of experience and particularly those with experience in a certain grade level or subject area. There is a bias that if candidates have experience, they are automatically better teachers. Although it may well be that the experienced candidate proves to be the top person for the position, we must not make that assumption based on experience alone. In fact, we both have hired first-year teachers who immediately made measurably positive impacts with students and on school culture.

People who are happy, successful, and making a significant difference tend to stay put in education.

When evaluating a candidate's experiences, the first question we need to ask ourselves is "Why are they looking for a position in the first place if it's a position similar to their current role?" Highly successful teachers are often happy in their current positions and schools. This is usually because they are achieving success and are being recognized for their efforts.

People who are happy, successful, and making a significant difference tend to stay put in education. Of course, there are numerous valid reasons for excellent people wanting to change positions, but it is important to learn *why* they want to leave their current role and to ensure they are not disgruntled or not working well with others.

Another drawback to consider when hiring based on a candidate's experience is the possibility that the experienced person already "knows" how everything is done or at least thinks they do. This is certainly not true of all experienced educators, but for some, years of successful experience may make them resistant to change. We want to avoid hiring someone who is going to be at odds with their team because they "have always done it this way."

When we examine a candidate's experience carefully, we can often discern their mindsets and talents. One piece of experience we sometimes find valuable is a candidate's experiences outside of education. This can be a strong indicator of mindset, interests, and future performance. Many people enter the education profession as a second career. In some instances, these folks have been in business yet felt a calling to become a teacher. Again, this is not the variable that will prove whether a candidate will be successful. Some who pursue teaching as a second career become outstanding educators, and others struggle when they leave the business world and enter our noble profession. Having said that, we do take time to consider candidates with experience outside of education. If the person possesses the right people skills and a genuine love for children and learning, it can be a valuable way to diversify our staff. A team staffed only with teachers who spent four years in college learning to be a teacher and then went directly to a classroom might be missing a broader perspective on how to approach challenges. By hiring people with experience in other industries, we may be able to add valuable perspectives. These individuals may be more outcomes-focused, and they may be inclined to view their job with a focus on *learning*, not just *teaching*.

Education and Training

Perhaps the least—or paradoxically, most—valuable aspect of any candidate profile is his or her education history. It is the most important because candidates must have at least a minimal amount of educational qualifications and certifications; however, it is also the least valuable because where someone attended school or what their Grade Point Average (GPA) was tells you very little about their future performance.

Where someone went to school is largely a factor of geography or their family's ability to pay tuition. We should not necessarily value one candidate over another because they went to one university over another. Where and how they accessed their education has very little to do with their potential to become a great teacher. In fact, some of the best teachers we know attended regional state schools and local colleges. At the same time, of course, there are outstanding teachers we know who attended rather prestigious schools. Much like the variable of experience, one's educational background is not a difference-maker in and of itself.

Not surprisingly, we have found that a candidate's GPA is yet another poor indicator of future performance as a teacher; in fact, it matters little to us if a candidate has a 4.0 or 2.0 GPA on a resume or application. A few years ago, in an interview with the *New York Times*, Laszlo Bock, then the vice president of People Operations at Google, said that GPAs and test scores are worthless criteria for hiring. Bock, now CEO and cofounder of the technology company Humu, explained that academic environments are largely artificial and not indicative of real work environments.

Being a teacher is very different from being a student. Just because a person learned to be successful in the system and environment of a university does not necessarily mean they will be successful in the work environment of a school. Using a candidate's GPA to tell us something about the potential of that candidate as a teacher is a dubious pursuit at best.

The training a candidate has had is more valuable than where someone attended school or what their GPA was. It can be valuable when a particular candidate has been trained in a certain program or process; for instance, if we are hiring a special education teacher and a candidate for the position has specific training in a reading program for students with dyslexia, that person may be a valuable addition to our special services team. If we are moving to a 1:1 learning environment at our school, a candidate who is an Apple or Google certified educator may be a great addition. Training still does not tell us much about whether someone will be truly successful, even though it can give us an indicator of what skills a person can bring to the table.

Talent

So what should we be hiring for when we have an open position? In a word, talent. We do not mean talent as something people are born with. To us, talent refers to a disposition, mindset, or overall character. In short, it is the way a person approaches the world. As principals, we always sought talented teachers of good character who were able to see more in their students than students saw in themselves combined with an ability to bring that greatness out. The reason we recruited such talented people is not only because they were better, but they were more likely to stay that way over time. We looked past experience and education, seeking to discern the "why?" of an individual. Why do they want to be a teacher? Why are they willing to work well beyond contractual hours to make a difference? Why do they want to be excellent? Experience and education can change over time, but who a person is, why they do what they do, and how they approach the world is likely to be the same in twenty years as it is today.

Talented teachers bridge the gap between the art and science of teaching to get the most out of their students.

Schools need teachers who are passionate about student learning and growth and who work tirelessly for the bigger picture of what our schools are all about. Talented teachers bridge the gap between the art and science of teaching to get the most out of their students. They work well with others. They do not have enormous egos and are willing to admit mistakes and reflect in order to improve. Talent is not hard to notice. Right now, you probably have in mind several people who fit the bill. You recognize them immediately as you read this; however, talent can be enormously difficult to identify in our current hiring practices where we only get to know a minimal amount about a person prior to offering them a position.

This is why we must work to ensure our hiring practices are about identifying talent. To do this means we may need to change our current practices. Principled principals have systems in place for hiring highly qualified *and* highly effective people. They know what true talent is all about and enlist a variety of resources to help them identify, recruit, and retain talented staff members. Great principals do not leave this important aspect of their job to chance and do not rely solely on any single variable when making hiring decisions.

Hiring versus Selection

All schools ultimately *hire* people, but some schools actually *select* people. There's a subtle difference between the two, and understanding this difference is the first step in "getting the right people on the bus," as Jim Collins calls it.

On the one hand, hiring people is an event: We have an opening and we need to fill it. But is there an actual hiring process in place with consistent practices and procedures that include various stakeholders' input? At some schools, the hiring process may be as simple as checking to see if the brother of one of our current employees wishes to join the team. At others, these processes are rigorous and focused on selecting talented people who will be a natural fit for the school culture which leaders seek to build. Like we said, all schools hire— some select.

When a school selects people, they are hiring with a more discerning eye that is focused on specific characteristics, such as talent. A process of selection helps us weed through applicants in a systematic way that is designed to help us identify the qualities we seek. To do this, we systematically employ processes and practices that help identify the right people. These processes and practices differ from school district to school district, and we have found several districts in the United States that do an excellent job in this area. These districts use different tools relating to application screening, interviewing, reference-checking, and even have prospective candidates teach a lesson as a way to show how they approach the classroom.

Although these hiring structures do vary, the key similarity is that they actually *exist* and are adhered to with fidelity. The only true variable between districts that consistently excel in this area and districts that do not is the fact that successful districts and school leaders have systems in place for selecting talented people, while less successful districts and school leaders leave this important aspect of our work to chance.

> **Principled principals make sure to select passionate people who are student focused and possess the right character for the school culture.**

There are numerous methods available to screen, interview, and ultimately select candidates for employment in our schools. Principled principals make sure to select passionate people who are student focused and possess the right character for the school culture. Although it is absolutely necessary to hire professional educators who possess knowledge and skills relating to the science of teaching, to a certain extent we consider this a given if they are deemed "highly qualified" in terms of state certification requirements. Even more important than hiring a passionate, highly *qualified teacher*, is hiring a passionate, highly *effective person* who is skilled in the art of teaching. Such candidates, quite honestly, would likely excel in any field, including The Four Seasons Hotel and Resort. Successful principals hire people first, knowing that if they select the right people, they can teach them specific skills they will need moving forward.

Input versus Decision

When hiring new staff members, we bring others into the process. When we hire teachers, we want other teachers to be involved and have a voice at the table; however, there is a big difference between having input and making decisions. There is only one person tasked with making the hiring decision, and that person is the principal. Everyone else should provide input to the principal to help make the best decision possible. We have seen some principals actually err on the side of being too inclusive in this area, hiring a candidate based on teacher preference, even though they may have doubts about whether the person is the best for the job. This is a mistake. Although we respect the input of every team member involved in the selection process and sincerely want their honest input, the principal is the ultimate gatekeeper determining who "gets in" as a staff member. Make the right decision and you have positively impacted lives of children and adults, hopefully for years to come. We have an obligation to our students, families, and community to make sure we select the best possible person. That means we take input but ultimately make the decision. Right or wrong, the principal is the person who will be held accountable for the decision. A fine line exists between being open and inclusive and handing over our responsibility to others.

The best way to establish this culture of input is to simply state your perspective honestly. For every open position at any school where we served, we invited a team of people to provide input. When we hire a third-grade teacher, we include other teachers from third grade, a special services teacher, and other personnel such as a music or art teacher or maybe an administrative assistant. At the beginning of the interview process, we clearly establish the expectations for the day and provide forms for each interviewing team member to provide their input. And we do make it clear that "input" is what we are seeking, as the final decision on whom to recommend will be made by the principal.

At the conclusion of the interviews, we rarely discuss the candidates as an interview team. Doing this has the potential to become an unstructured airing of opinions where the conversation is dominated by the loudest voices or strongest personalities; instead, we collect input sheets, poring over them meticulously to understand interview team members' thoughts and impressions.

If we adhere to this process and clearly establish the difference between providing input versus making the ultimate decision, team members tend to embrace the opportunity to be heard and respect the principal's accountability. In addition, we find that we receive more thoughtful input from written feedback forms than we do from open discussion. This process allows us to evaluate each candidate as objectively as possible.

The "Gut Instinct" Factor

If there is anything we hope you take away from this chapter, it's this: Principals need a systematic, consistent process to help identify highly qualified, highly effective, and talented individuals. Having said that, we must not leave our human judgment out of such processes.

There are instances when we should listen to our "gut instinct." Sometimes we simply have a feeling that someone will be a perfect fit, or conversely, we get the feeling that someone is just not quite right for our school. These are real impressions that should not be ignored. Either instance, however, will likely evidence itself during the interview, and others on the team will likely feel the same, making our decision obvious. Structured systems become even more crucial, in this context, to eliminate potential bias. When we have a process with multiple components, we buy ourselves the freedom to go with our "gut" during the in-person interviews.

In his excellent book *The Advantage*, Patrick Lencioni dedicates just a few pages to recruiting and hiring. Although this section comprises a tiny portion of his book and was not written for hiring teachers, it is well worth reading. In particular, he cautions against going with your "gut feel" and argues against those who believe they can make effective hiring decisions without hiring structures. At the same time, he concludes the section by arguing against an overly-structured hiring process:

"The best approach to hiring people is to put just enough structure in place to ensure a measure of consistency and adherence to core values—and no more. That's right. When it comes to the continuum of hiring, ironically, I find that it is better to be somewhere closer to having a little less structure than more. I believe this because too much structure almost always interferes with a person's ability to use their common sense, and it is far easier to add a little structure later to a fairly bare system than it is to deconstruct an already over complicated process."

As school leaders, we can agree or disagree with Lencioni about where our practices stand on the continuum, ranging from very little structure to very rigid structures. Great principals have systems in place that allow them to select for excellence.

The Talent Principle
3-2-1

3

PRINCIPALS' PERSPECTIVES ON THE TALENT PRINCIPLE

Amber Teamann (@8Amber8) is principal of Whitt Elementary in Wylie (TX) ISD. From serving as a fourth-grade teacher at a public-school technology center to her role as a Title I Technology Facilitator responsible for seventeen campuses, Amber has helped students and staff navigate their digital abilities and responsibilities. Through her campus-level leadership, she has helped initiate change district wide, empowering teachers at all levels. Amber knows the importance of seeking out team members who are not only excellent but who also complement the skill sets of other team members:

> I am a big believer in surrounding myself with people who are smarter than me. While that may seem intimidating, let me explain. When I use the word "smarter," I mean that I look for skill sets or perspectives that I don't have. My favorite leadership team with whom I have had the opportunity to work consisted of what I like to refer to as our "triage" of leaders. I was the "activator," as the one who turned thoughts into actions. I also had a "processor" on my team; he was the one who wanted to think things through and take his time. He came up with some very forward-thinking

117

ideas, and his vision for where we "could be" was what helped drive our campus. Finally, we had an "includer." Her grasp of others and their feelings ensured we covered all the bases. There wasn't a chance of us leaving someone out or missing a detail when we had the three of us in the room making decisions for our campus.

Those relationships taught me there is value in looking at what others bring to the table. When I think of hiring for our campus now, I think of adding value that will balance out our existing team. Leverage one's "weaknesses" as strengths when you can; for example, a team member who might be considered "negative" may simply be quite analytical and offer perspective you have not considered.

I tell every staff member I hire that I want my campus to be more like them than I want them to be like my campus. There is some spark, some energy, some skill they have that I would love to see emulated within our team. That is what you are looking for when you hire, something that will make your campus stronger. Don't seek to bring people who are just like you to your team; you want complementary skills. This will make everyone better!

David Geurin (@DavidGeurin) is principal of Bolivar High School, a National Blue Ribbon High School in Missouri. He was recently recognized as a 2017 National Association of Secondary School Principals (NASSP) Digital Principal of the Year. David understands that hiring for excellence is critical to student success and approaches the hiring and retaining aspects of his job with intention. Here David shares a few of his thoughts on hiring and retaining excellent staff members:

If we are going to create an amazing school, we need to recruit and retain amazing educators. We involve a committee in this process at our school. We want to have a variety of perspectives in making these decisions. We have teacher leaders, instructional coaches, counselors, and others at the table providing feedback on our candidates. At times we've asked candidates to prepare and teach a model lesson for us. We ask questions that try to go deeper and require more than canned responses. We are also interested to see what questions the candidates will ask us. That can reveal underlying priorities and assumptions also.

I am looking to hire individuals who are passionate about learning and who are passionate about kids. I don't care as much about what they know right now as long as I know they are deeply invested and are eager to learn. I look for evidence they did more than expected in their previous teaching assignment or in their teacher preparation program. I consider how I think they would connect with others. What kind of teammate would they be?

It's also important to see how their philosophy fits with the vision for our school. For us, that means we are looking for them to embrace a digital learning culture. We want them to design learning experiences, not just lessons. We want to see authentic work and not just quizzes or tests. I often use the interview or a follow-up meeting to discuss expectations so they can start to envision how they will fit into our school's mission.

Of course, it's just as important to retain great teachers as it is to hire them. We strive to create a culture of teamwork and togetherness. Occasionally a teacher may leave us because of life circumstances or retirement, but it won't be because they didn't love it here. That happens when you value people, show appreciation, and support them in doing meaningful work.

Jonathan Howell (@fris_trex) has been in education for the past twenty-three years as a classroom teacher, head baseball coach, and school administrator. He is currently principal at Fossil Ridge Intermediate, a sixth- and seventh-grade school in St. George, Utah. Fossil Ridge is nationally recognized by Solution Tree as a "Model Professional Learning Community (PLC)" school, and NASSP as a "National Breakthrough" school. Jonathan shares his wisdom about not only hiring and retaining talented staff members but also relying on these talented people to help lead the school:

> While lying in bed one night, I began to focus on our data collection process at Fossil Ridge. What could I do to improve the way we used our assessment data? As I thought more about it, I had what seemed like an epiphany. I thought my idea was fabulous, and I believed it would change the way we looked at data at Fossil Ridge. The next day I shared my idea with the faculty and gave them direction to move forward. The teachers looked horrified, upset, and confused, but I didn't really understand why.
>
> What happened over the course of the next few days was nothing short of a disaster! My wonderful idea had flopped, and in the meantime, I had broken the trust and confidence of our teachers.
>
> Where had I gone wrong? I did not talk to our data experts, I did not solicit the help or advice of any faculty member. I did not take the idea to the Leadership Team. I went in alone and failed miserably. I learned a hard but powerful lesson: It was clear that I needed to discover our talent, rely on that talent, and use the talent all around me to build a culture of excellence at Fossil Ridge.
>
> We were able to initiate this process by focusing on two critical ideas: First, it was imperative that we find and use the talent that was already present at Fossil Ridge to improve our school. Second, and I believe this to be one of the most important things we do as principals, we had to intentionally hire and retain "rock star" educators who were passionate, enthusiastic, and willing to share their unique talents. As we went about more successfully incorporating shared leadership at our school, I quickly learned that I was not, nor would I ever be, the smartest person in the room.
>
> I made it a personal goal to eliminate the words "I," "Me," and "Mine" from my educational vocabulary. It isn't shared responsibility if it's all about me. It isn't shared leadership if I take the credit for our successes, and it isn't "talent sharing" if I fail to recognize the amazing contributions of the people working in the trenches.

A culture of "talent sharing" is absolutely vital to the effectiveness of a principal, but more importantly, it is vital to the overall success and morale of the school. As principals, we must have the courage to let go, the foresight to employ the unique talents of our faculty members, and the judgment to hire teachers that will transform teaching and learning in our schools. There's talent all around you. Go find it. Be excellent!

2

TALENT PRINCIPLE RESOURCES

For a list of these and other resources, please visit **theprincipledprincipal.com.**

"First Impressions Matter"

We love this post about the hiring process from Jimmy Casas, longtime principal at Bettendorf High School in Iowa. Casas says that although some administrators might prefer to bypass the work involved in hiring new teachers, he genuinely looks forward to it. In this post, he shares seven of his best practices related to the hiring process.

eX Factor Foundational Five[SM]

(principles.humanexventures.com)

This short survey from Humanex Ventures will give you a quick snapshot of your foundational five talents. It is important to lead from strengths-based positions, not only for staff but also for yourself. This quick survey will help identify your talents.

1

TALENT PRINCIPLE CULTURE CRUSHER

When school leaders do not have norms, expectations, structures, processes, and procedures established for how to behave when difficult situations arise, we are destroying the culture of that school. Although we may not immediately think of hiring staff as an example of a "difficult situation arising in our school," conducted poorly, the hiring process can indeed be a difficult situation for all stakeholders. Regardless of the current status of the school culture, each time we bring a new member onto the team, the culture will be impacted. It is our responsibility to ensure that it is impacted in a positive direction.

For this reason, principled principals ensure that structured hiring practices are in place at the school; moreover, they ensure that everyone in the school is aware of these structures and knows why they are important. There are no surprises when it comes to hiring new staff. Everyone on the team knows what they are looking for and how they will go about identifying and attracting the candidates most likely to bring what is needed to the school.

One final element that excellent principals make known to both veteran and new staff members when it comes to hiring is this: Although they clearly seek to hire new staff members who will "fit" with the current culture, they also seek to hire new staff members who bring "missing pieces" to the school. "Fit" works both ways. Great principals expect new teachers to push the culture in new and better ways.

PRINCIPLE 6
The Change Principle

The question, then, is not whether one accepts
the responsibility. Just by doing this work,
one has. The question is, having accepted the
responsibility, how one does such work well.

—*Atul Gawande*

The quote above from surgeon and author Atul Gawande perfectly sums up our view on change. Gawande primarily writes about medicine and his learnings from the field of healthcare, but his insights are as applicable to education as they are to surgery. Just as surgeons accept the incredible responsibility of having people's lives in their hands, we, as teachers and leaders in education, accept the responsibility for the children we serve.

As Gawande says, the true question is *how* we will do our work well. As educators, we have a responsibility to continually ask this question. How do we do our work well—and better than we did it last week and last year? This must always be our starting point when thinking about change. Change has, or should have, a purpose: to improve what we currently do. Of course, change can take many forms: a new reading curriculum, a new electronic resource to use with students, a new social emotional program, or staffing changes, yet any change we implement should be guided by our desire to improve, to do new and better things, and to do what we currently do . . . better.

A decade ago, John Kotter explained that we are moving from a state of episodic change to a state of continuous change. We can think of episodic change as sporadic events, with breaks in between. An example of episodic change in education might be adopting the new math curriculum once every five years. After that curriculum adoption, everyone would adjust and then relax back into a mostly traditional approach to teaching and learning. The desks all still faced the front of the room, the teacher probably still lectured from the board, and homework was still that worksheet, but from the new curriculum resources.

If we are not constantly changing, we are probably missing something.

Continuous change, on the other hand, means a constant state of flux in one area or another. Without an effective principal leading continuous change, others in the school may become overwhelmed. It seems as if there is always something new facing us. Whether we are talking about a new app or learning resource, new research on best practices, or even new state laws impacting our work, we are inundated with ideas for changing our current practices. Forget the new curriculum adoption; just working in a school today feels like we are in a constant state of change. And that is the point. Ten years ago, Kotter said we were moving to a continuous state of change. Today, it is clear we have arrived.

If we are not constantly changing, we are probably missing something, since human knowledge is doubling every year. Shockingly, at the end of World War II, the rate was every twenty-five years. Moreover, IBM predicts that we are headed to a reality where the amount of human knowledge doubles every twelve hours. People learning about developing an app for the iPad may very well find that their learning becomes obsolete in less than a year. As difficult as this reality is, educators must constantly imagine a world in which much of what we learn today is no longer relevant tomorrow. It is for these reasons that schools must embrace, not resist, change. Great principals not only embrace change themselves, they also help others embrace change as opportunities to serve our students better.

Leading change successfully starts by being honest with our colleagues and explaining why a continuous state of change is our new reality. We know there are people in our schools who long for more quiet and simple times. Sometimes we agree. But for better or worse, those days are not coming back, and it behooves us as leaders to serve as change trailblazers rather than change resistors. Our kids need us to prepare them for an ever-changing world.

Recently we were talking to a group of teachers who told us they liked all the positive changes happening in their school but wished they could just take a break and not do anything new for a year or so. These happened to be people we consider excellent educators and leaders. The first thing we have to accept as change agents is that a desire to slow the change process is a common and natural feeling. Being in a state of continuous change means that being a teacher tomorrow is a little bit different, or more difficult, than it was today. But it can also become more rewarding, efficient, and impactful.

As we listened to these teachers, we validated their feelings. As former teachers ourselves, we are not immune to those feelings; however, we also explained why we needed to accept the reality in which we work. One reason we cannot slow down is because the world is not slowing down. We owe it to our students to be on the cutting edge of learning and innovation. We are preparing them for a world that does not yet exist. The truth is, education is not the same as it was ten, twenty, or thirty years ago. In fact, it is not the same as it was even two years ago.

Of course, it is not enough for principals to simply talk about change. Yes, one of the first things great principals do is orient their staff to this new reality. The key to leading successful change lies in how we manage the process. Without the correct approach and skilled management of change, principals find themselves becoming what Michael Fullan calls "dead right." By this he means we may be 100 percent correct about the changes that need to be made and the steps needed to get us there, but instead of staff, parents, and students jumping right in to follow our lead, we are met with opposition at every turn.

Great principals embrace change and instill a sense of urgency regarding the need for change within those they lead. They also support students, staff, and parents throughout the journey.

Embrace the Process

More and more principals serve in districts equipped with 1:1 learning environments. As technology tools become more affordable and the educational need for it is enhanced, it makes sense that schools are finding ways to put a device in every student's hand. Planning, implementing, and monitoring a 1:1 learning initiative in your school or district is one of the most significant changes schools can make. It impacts everything from how learning should occur daily in the classroom to whether students take devices home to behind-the-scenes systems management issues. Making the transition to a 1:1 learning school or district is a huge disruption to the status quo.

Responses to making this transition vary widely when we talk to teachers, parents, and principals. We have spoken to some who described it as the greatest change they ever made. In these schools and districts, there has been overwhelming support and positive feedback. On the other hand, in some places, this very same change has been a disaster for teachers and families. In these schools, teachers and families see no benefit, are not using the devices to their full potential, and it seems to be creating more problems than solutions. In extreme cases, we have even heard of schools reversing course on this change, moving away from devices for all students.

Whether change is received well or poorly is much less about the change itself and much more about how the change is managed.

How can the same change be so successful in some schools and so unsuccessful in others? In some instances, schools within the very same district sometimes have distinctly divergent responses to the implementation. We believe it comes down to the change *process*. Whether change is received well or poorly is much less about the change itself and much more about how the change is managed. This is where great principals succeed and mediocre principals fail. We all know we need to change and do things better, but how we move through that process is where success—or failure—truly resides.

Author and consultant William Bridges suggests, "It isn't the changes that do you in; it's the transitions." In his book *Managing Transitions*, Bridges explains that change is situational. Today there is one reality; tomorrow there will be a different one. Transitioning is psychological in that it includes the process of letting go of the old reality and embracing the new reality. Changes, even welcome ones, are not immune to psychological responses among those affected.

Start with Why

One of the first steps great principals take when implementing change is clarifying *why* we need to change in the first place. This requires not a passing mention of the why, but a deep exploration of the need for the change, asking, *Why this? Why now? Why not?* Principled principals ensure the change process begins on the path to success by investing a significant amount of time establishing the why.

Although change is constant, we should not be afraid to let it take its time, and we should rule, rather than be ruled by, any changes coming our way. One district we know spent more than a year planning for their transition to a 1:1 learning environment, ensuring they had established the why with staff, students, parents, and board members. The superintendent, assistant superintendent, principals, and assistant principals held regular conversations with teachers and other staff members, both formally and informally, more than a year in advance of the implementation. The conversations were not about a predetermined future of becoming a 1:1 school district; rather, they were focused on the need to transform learning for students.

The district gained commitment to the change process by talking about why this would be better for students. And they took their time. Pilot classrooms, opportunities for teachers to visit pilot classrooms, and after-school workshops for teachers and families were also part of the district's process. By the time they actually moved forward with a 100 percent adoption for all students in all grades, every stakeholder was fully informed and prepared for the change, including those who were most against it at the outset.

Whatever changes we may implement, we must make sure to start with the why.

Whatever changes we may implement, we must make sure to start with the why. In doing so, great principals focus on why the idea is better for their most important customers: every student at their school.

Be Honest

It has been nearly a decade since the release of the Common Core State Standards (CCSS) in math and English language arts, yet we are surprised how many schools are only now beginning to understand the demands of these new learning standards. Although there exist a host of possible reasons many schools have failed to implement the Common Core fully and successfully, we believe it begins with one word: honesty.

When the Common Core State Standards were released, they represented a sea of change in the way we think about teaching and learning. But some of the most beneficial aspects of the standards are found in their introduction and appendix sections. These sections explain the research behind the standards and new models of learning. Many people, however, skipped these sections entirely and went directly to their grade-level standards, not understanding the underlying philosophical shifts and how significantly these would impact instruction when implemented with fidelity.

Part of the blame for not having a smoother and swifter transition to the new standards was the fact that many educators had not taken the time to simply read the documents carefully. Another reason lies in the fact that many of us were not completely honest with ourselves.

We remember sitting in meetings when the CCSS were released and hearing about the "shifts," which was inevitably followed by someone suggesting, "We are already doing a lot of this; this isn't really a huge change. We don't need to worry." But nothing could be further from the truth. The Common Core turned everything we had been doing on its head. This is the message people should have received, but it was not the message many school leaders sent.

Our suspicion, as is so often the case in schools, is that we were afraid of pushing too far, too fast. School leaders were afraid of making the change seem dramatically different from the status quo and sought to downplay potential implications of the Common Core. The results? Nearly a decade of mostly half-implemented and stalled changes in school districts across the country.

It has taken years for educators to realize that the Common Core is based on an entirely different concept of what rigorous reading and writing looks like. Even today, far too many educators do not truly understand the new standards. Again, one simple reason is they were not told the truth about the change. The impact of adopting the CCSS was minimized at every turn in many schools. As people began to discover this was more than a simple "shift," they began to revolt. As a result, entire states have abandoned their adoption of the CCSS, and the struggle for full implementation continues.

The lesson for us is to always be honest about change. We should never sugar-coat change or make it seem like it's something it is not. We believe good people never shy away from hard work and are almost always willing to enact change if they are told the truth about why it matters and what it involves. When it comes to change, what people desire most is simply to know what is coming. They crave a certainty in understanding what the future will look like. Great principals do not downplay change; they are honest and transparent about what the change will entail.

Personalize Involvement

When implementing change, it is important for principals to fully understand the process themselves and teach others thoroughly. They must also make certain that people understand exactly what roles they will play throughout the process. Large-scale changes such as a curriculum adoption, 1:1 learning environments, and moving from traditional to flexible seating involve almost everyone in the school, although what is needed from each individual may vary. If we are implementing 1:1 learning, the role in the change process is very different depending on whether we are a classroom teacher, a technology director, an instructional coach, special education teacher, principal, or speech pathologist.

Everyone should know the scope of the change process and what it will look like. But how each individual fits in and contributes to the process must be personalized. In addition, we should provide all people some amount of choice about what roles they will play in the process as it moves forward. Personalizing the change process increases the likelihood others will commit to the change both during the process and after the change; for instance, a speech pathologist may need support in understanding how a 1:1 learning environment can help him or her deliver services better. The answer may be having students using apps on a tablet, or a computer on which to practice at home. It may be having students record their pronunciation as a way for them to get immediate feedback.

> **Personalizing the change process increases the likelihood others will commit to the change both during the process and after the change.**

We make crucial errors when we assume staff members will magically figure out "all the great things change will bring" on their own. Some will, but our responsibility is to support everyone from their personal "Point A" to their "Point B." Great principals help people see how change will impact the school as a whole and how it will make them better in their individual roles.

Communicate Change

One of the most important things great principals do throughout the change process is communicate the change.

This happens even before the change process technically begins, during the process itself, and after the change has been fully implemented. When communicating, it is important to understand we are interacting with many different audiences, and the message needs to be tailored as such. What a parent needs to know about the process of change may be different than that of a student or a teacher. While the message may be similar, we need to design it to speak specifically to that group. But the "why" will be the same whether we are communicating to students, staff, or parents.

If we continue using our example of transitioning to 1:1 learning for all, we must consider that teachers and parents may have very different concerns about this initiative when deciding what, when, and how to communicate. A teacher's concerns may center on how it will change instruction: Will it help or hurt learning? How will it impact this unit or lesson? How will I learn to integrate technology effectively in my daily instruction? Parents may share some of these same concerns, but it is likely that, if you are sending devices home, parents' more immediate concerns are not what their students are doing with the devices at school but what they are doing with them at home. Parents want to know if there are filters on the devices to block inappropriate content or what the recommended amount of time on the devices is for their children. These are legitimate questions that schools must address.

Great principals are excellent communicators who know how to anticipate the concerns of their stakeholders and learn their concerns. Great principals are great empathizers who are able to put themselves into the shoes of their parents, teachers, and students and then speak to those differing perspectives.

How's the Weather?

We have all heard the phrase, "If you don't like the weather, wait fifteen minutes." Although we imagine many people think the saying is native to their city, state, or region, it seems every place we visit around the country uses this saying about their local weather. Jeff once heard someone say this in Las Vegas in the middle of July when the temperature was about 115 degrees, and it hadn't rained in a month. This phrase has been used for decades, often attributed to Mark Twain talking about the weather in New England. The fact that so many people seem to identify with this saying is a testament to our ever-changing world. Our perception as humans is that our personal world and our surroundings are ever changing and that this is unsettling. Yet, unlike the weather in Las Vegas, the reality is that little in our lives is stoic and stagnant. In this context, it is important to remember the best approach as a leader is to be perfectly comfortable basking in the sunlight or dancing in the rain and letting others know they will be fine too. We cannot let the fact that there is change in our professional lives dictate our attitude and approaches to our work any more than we can allow changes in the weather to do so.

Great principals embrace and model this attitude in their schools. Change is not something to fear or from which to run. It is part of a natural process, as natural as the changing weather. If people we lead already feel like their surroundings are ever-changing, the best approach is to embrace the reality and attempt to steer attitudes in the right direction. Principled principals lean into the winds of change.

The Change Principle
3-2-1

3

PRINCIPALS' PERSPECTIVES ON THE CHANGE PRINCIPLE

Beth Houf (@BethHouf) is a middle school principal in central Missouri. She also serves as a facilitator for the Department of Elementary and Secondary Education (DESE) Leadership Academy, providing monthly training to state educational leaders. She has spoken at the International Society for Technology in Education (ISTE) Conference, the Association for Middle Level Education National Conference and many state and local educational venues. She is a National Distinguished Principal and coauthor of *LEAD Like a PIRATE*. Beth knows that change is a process, not an event, and shares tips for leading change successfully:

> Change is a process, not a one-time event. To lead change, you must anticipate and understand how change impacts people, and that means being strategic as you plan for change.
>
> Get clear about the expectations you have for the change, then carefully consider the systems of support you will need to provide for people as you ask them to do some of their work differently. As leaders, we must build the compelling "why" for the change and anticipate those that ask, "Why not stick with what

135

we are already doing?"

Change for change's sake or change without a really good reason behind it will get you nowhere. In order to make this happen, change isn't something you announce from the podium at a staff meeting. Change builds over time. If you want to implement something new and make it amazing, you have to put in the time and build the foundation to make it happen. Get your crew involved in making the change a reality. People are less likely to tear down systems they help to build.

How do you make this happen? My first step is to find a colleague outside of my building from whom I can elicit feedback about my thoughts regarding potential changes. It is helpful to have a person who isn't closely involved in the change initiative to hear the initial idea before I take it to the building level. This helps me to be better focused as well as get a different perspective. I then brainstorm with as many stakeholders as possible who will be involved in making the change a reality. What could the change look like? What shouldn't it look like? What are potential roadblocks? How could we remove them? What are the benefits of the change? Are there other ideas to consider? After you have had the chance to brainstorm, take the data gathered from staff to a smaller group (e.g., the school leadership team) to disaggregate. This group can help you find out if you need to get more information and pave the way for next steps.

When stakeholders are involved, it becomes "our change," not the principal's change, which drives ownership and a greater likelihood for success.

Winston Sakurai (@WinstonSakurai) has distinguished himself as an innovative educational leader at the state and national level for over twenty-five years. In 1993, at the age of twenty, he was appointed to the Hawaii State Board of Education and served multiple terms as vice chairperson. He was recently named by the National Association of Secondary School Principals as a 2016 National Digital Principal of the Year and by the Hawaii Association of Secondary School Administrators as the 2016 Hawaii State Secondary Principal of the Year. Winston compares the skill of preparing for change to the way chess players must anticipate and plan:

> Mention "change," and some people cringe. Sometimes their hands go up, either literally or figuratively as a mental block. In education, where trends come and go and the pendulum of ideas swings the full gamut, veteran educators can feel like they have seen it all—not to mention that sticking with what currently works is often easier. The idea, "If it isn't broken, why fix it?" does not always apply to education when we are tasked with raising up future generations of leaders.
>
> The curricular constraints of time are a real challenge for everyone on a school campus, so asking people to change becomes a task, but it's also a wonderful opportunity that needs to be done purposefully. That is why change-leadership is crucial to the success of any healthy school.
>
> As we have seen by the downfall of the Blockbuster video stores, being resistant to change, not seeing where the market is going, and not knowing what consumers want can lead to the ruin of an organization. That is why I have found we need to constantly look to the future to understand what needs to change today. As with playing chess, we must see how the future moves we make will lead to a checkmate while anticipating the different scenarios that can play out.
>
> It is vital to be the change you want to see in your organization. Modeling change for our faculty and staff helps them see the change in action. That means continuously learning and growing as a professional: being humble and showing we don't know it all, taking risks and having a growth mindset, and knowing that not all the things we implement will work. Change begins with

the leader first. We have to be willing to change in order to help others successfully change for the better.

It is essential to my practice as a change leader to be a connected leader. Technology has reinvented the playing field and multiplied the pace at which change happens. Forming a strong network of other forward-thinking change leaders is crucial. I am able to gain many insights and ideas from the collective thoughts of the best educational minds out there. Utilizing the technology available today, I am able to instantly connect with people around the globe, even as I lead a school in the middle of the Pacific Ocean. Technology has overcome geography when it comes to connecting people.

We must create environments in which change is embraced, people are on board, and momentum is continuous. Being empathetic to how change initiatives affect the school by monitoring and understanding how people are feeling is key to the long-term health of the organization.

Jethro Jones (@jethrojones) is principal of Tanana Middle School in Fairbanks, Alaska, and the NASSP 2017 Digital Principal of the Year. He is the host of the *Transformative Principal* podcast and the Transformative Leadership Summit. His goal is to impact one hundred million students by 2027 by helping school leaders improve their schools. He believes the best way to educate is to give learners what they need when they need it. Jethro knows that in education, regardless of our role, we are in the people business. As such, we are in the change business since, thankfully, people are constantly growing:

A teacher once asked me why things change so much. "Why can't we just say we are good enough at X and not keep changing things?" she lamented. I asked her if she ever had the same class two years in a row. Of course, she didn't. I asked her if her class ever changed throughout the year. She admitted that it did. I told her that as educators, we are working with people, first and foremost, and people, thankfully, are constantly evolving and growing.

Every situation impacts us and changes us. So as educators, we are constantly exposed to that change. Early in my career, I was pushing for improvement. The staff saw that as "change" but not necessarily as an opportunity for positive growth. As I took on the new principal role, a domino effect began: The whole office staff turned over as well. People who had been at that school for years decided to move on to other opportunities.

Instead of fearing change, I encouraged the teachers and staff to embrace this complete turnover in the front office as a time to start anew, to define themselves and our school in whatever ways they wanted. Why does everything always change? Because we are in the people business, and rather than fear change, we would be well-served to embrace it, prepare for it, and make it successful.

2

CHANGE PRINCIPLE RESOURCES

For a list of these and other resources,
please visit theprincipledprincipal.com.

"4 Things Successful Change Leaders Do Well"
Recognize embedded tensions and paradoxes. Hold everyone accountable. Invest in new organizational capabilities.
Emphasize continuous learning. Read more in this excellent
article posted in the Harvard Business Review.

"Leading Change: 35 Questions to Ask First"
This article includes thirty-five questions you must ask when
leading change. Although geared toward the business world, it
also applies to education and includes several video links, an
infographic, and links to additional resources on change.

1

CHANGE PRINCIPLE
CULTURE CRUSHER

When school leaders allow too much time for staff members to push back against change, sharing why they are opposed and why it will not work at "our" school, we are destroying the culture of that school. Here are three culture-crushing staff members to be on the lookout for. Try to anticipate their complaints as well as your response:

Mr. "But That's the Way We Have Always Done It"

Mr. BTTWWHADI is a culture crusher. He believes the status quo is good enough, and what worked last year—or twenty years ago—will always be the best approach. Our response should focus on the fact that new and better ways are constantly being invented in every industry and education should be as innovative—if not more innovative—than any other industry.

The CYBO (Chief "Yeah, But" Officer)

Ms. CYBO often begins her pushback with the words, "Yeah, but…" and frequently follows this with "We tried this before and it did not work." Be prepared to learn from the CYBO about what was tried, when it was tried, and why it failed, explaining how this situation is different and reminding her that if it is best for kids, we never give up trying to find new ways to do our work.

Dr. "But What If"

Dr. But What If may be partially willing to commit but wants to remind us of the perils, often asking, "But what if we do this and (fill in the blank here with any number of horrific possible outcomes) happens?" Dr. But What If is incessantly focused on what *might* go wrong. Be prepared to admit that things may go wrong, particularly during the implementation dip, but flip the question with this person, asking, "But what if we do nothing and miss out on what could be an amazing difference maker for students and staff at our school?"

Note that all three staff members have the word "But" in their names. When it comes to change in schools, culture crushers often invoke this word. Principled principals build the culture by allowing everyone on staff to have their voice heard while also letting everyone know when the time for debate has ceased and the time for action has begun.

PRINCIPLE 7
The Communication Principle

The art of communication is the language of leadership.

—*James Humes*

C ommunication is not only one of the 4 Cs of twenty-first-century learning, it is also one of the most important responsibilities of a school leader. Good communication keeps staff, students, parents, and community members in the loop of the school's business and is a major factor in garnering support.

Regardless of how well intentioned, poor communication can sabotage any initiative. In addition, inadequate communication is probably the most common reason principals lose their jobs. Far more principals are done in by poor relationship and communication skills than poor test scores. Great principals are dynamic and innovative communicators who are not only aware of the specific message they are trying to convey; they are also aware of the big-picture story their school must tell.

All Schools Tell a Story

We all have a story to tell. Every staff member and student in your school, every parent in your community, and every principal in every school has a story. But schools tell stories too. Schools tell the story of a community. This includes not only the current state of affairs but also the community's hopes and dreams for the future. In many cities, towns, and villages, the school is the hub of the community that links all its members to a common experience. The feeling in a school and the message of a school is often a reflection of the community itself. A school, however, can be much more than a reflection; it can lead a community by supporting priorities and values. A school is this important. *Your* school is this important. A school is, of course, a place where children come to learn and grow. More important still, it is a place where parents and the community send their hopes and dreams for the future. Understanding this is crucial to communicating with the big picture in mind.

Because the school is such an integral part of the community, it can also become a prime target for criticism, complaints, and concern within the community. Regardless of the amazing things that might be happening in your school, someone can find something to complain about. As principals, we have found that some of the complaints actually had very little to do with the school.

We've had meetings with parents whose primary concern involved a situation between adults in their neighborhood and had nothing to do with their children or the school. Although not every concern that made its way into our offices was a school concern, the fact that someone would bring a non-school issue to a principal's attention shows how important the school is to a community. As principals, we must be sensitive to this reality. Every time principals speak to a parent, they are not merely communicating with that one person. Messages pass from person to person throughout the community. Great principals know that when they speak to one parent, they're speaking to the entire community.

Great principals know that when they speak to one parent, they're speaking to the entire community.

The same could be said regarding discussions with staff members. When sharing a message with one teacher, be prepared for it to spread—accurately or not—to the entire staff. This can work to our advantage when the message is relatively easy and our decisions on issues are met with widespread support. But what about when you must stand your ground with a parent over a sensitive issue or with a staff member about a non-negotiable instructional issue? The message that is spread about you and your school may not be as widely supported by others who hear it second hand. This is why telling your school's story through proactive communication makes a difference.

To illustrate, let's use a common example of a hot topic in schools today: bullying. The Department of Health and Human Services defines bullying as "Unwanted aggressive behavior among school aged children that involves a real or perceived power imbalance. The behavior is repeated, or has the potential to be repeated, over time." Bullying is a significant problem in our schools, and it is our responsibility to protect students from not only traditional bullying behavior, such as verbal and physical abuse, but also cyberbullying. One of our most important jobs, if not *the* most important job, is the safety of our students. But what, exactly, constitutes bullying? Does it include every mean word that might be said by a five-year-old towards another student? Of course it doesn't, but not everyone perceives such instances the same way.

Anyone who has served as a school administrator is likely familiar with such scenarios. The parent of a second-grade student comes into your office visibly agitated about an incident involving his or her son at school. Another child had called him a name at recess, and the child was hurt by the words. The parent insists this is a clear instance of "bullying" and that the other student must be dealt with as a "bully." This parent insists the other child's parents be brought in immediately to be reprimanded for their child's behavior. You assure the parent that you will investigate and get back to them. The parent agrees to let you look into it and departs but not before again demanding the school take swift and stern action.

As you investigate the matter and talk to both children, you do, in fact, discover that one student called the other a name at recess. These are two children who often play together and acknowledge each other as friends. While talking to the student who was called the name, you see that the boy was clearly hurt because his friend called him a bad name. While talking to the "perpetrator," you explain how that made the other child feel. The offending child begins to express remorse, apologizes to the other child, and the apology is accepted. The children go to recess, and you commit yourself to monitoring the situation closely in the days ahead to ensure there is nothing more sinister going on beneath the surface, and this was simply an isolated incident. Although you deem it appropriate to continue monitoring the situation closely, your investigation reveals this is clearly not an incident of bullying.

You then call the parents of the offending child and explain to them what happened. They thank you and say they will discuss it at home with their son as well. You also, of course, contact the parent who visited your office and explain the situation and the resolution. In many cases, this is where this story ends: The parent thanks you for taking care of the situation.

As principals, we take all sides of the story into account and keep the big picture in mind.

Alas, not all stories have such endings. At times, despite the actions you have taken, the parent is not happy. Instead of thanking you for your involvement, you are accused of not taking bullying seriously, and your school is accused of not being sensitive to students who are being bullied. You listen calmly, as the parent paints a picture of your school as a heartless place (or as one parent once suggested to us, a school that is "soft on crime"). In such instances, the only outcome that would satisfy the parent would be suspending or expelling the alleged bully. Although such a response may seem irrational to us as school leaders, it also requires us to be empathetic. As principals, we take all sides of the story into account and keep the big picture in mind. Parents have a clear vested interest in one party: their own child. It is upsetting to see your child hurt in any way. We understand. Yet we still have an obligation to examine every situation from a larger perspective.

The phone conversation ends with the parent threatening that this is not the end of the story. They may talk to other parents, the superintendent, and maybe even the school board. "A school that tolerates bullying is unacceptable, and the community needs to be aware of this," the parent says before hanging up the phone. Clearly, this parent is angry and will share their concerns in the community. This parent has the ability to say whatever they want and you are defenseless to rebut any false claims, as this is an internal, confidential matter of student behavior. As the principal of a school, there is no public trial when there is a disagreement among students or parents. The only defense you have is the story you've been telling about your school.

Let's consider this same situation in the case of a principal who is a great communicator, and one who is not so great.

A great principal feels confident because they consistently shared what the school is doing for the social, emotional health of its students, including communicating regularly with families about the classroom lessons implemented to prevent bullying. Prior to this incident, the principal has also communicated the decline in the reported incidents of bullying at the school over the past year. The principal also regularly shares examples of students working together to solve problems. The school has taken great steps to ensure an inclusive environment which minimizes bullying among students. The principal communicates this through newsletters, emails, at regularly-scheduled parent nights, during informal conversations with parents, and on new mediums such as Twitter and Facebook; in fact, if you were to go into the community and speak to parents about bullying at the school, they would likely be able to name several steps the school has taken to prevent bullying as well as the decline in bullying incidents. In this case, the school and principal have done a great job of proactively telling their story of inclusion and prevention. Even though we have an upset parent who's sharing her story with anyone who will listen, our own story is already firmly rooted in the community and will likely prevail over a lone voice.

A principal with poor communication practices might be in some trouble in this situation. This is true even if they have done all the wonderful things mentioned above to prevent bullying. But if no one knows about these efforts, negativity can prevail. It is nearly impossible to change a narrative after a story has been written.

As the angry parent begins to spread their frustration in the community, this principal begins getting phone calls from other parents. PTO board members demand a meeting because it seems there is a systemic problem of bullying at the school. At the meeting, the principal tries to explain all the things the school has done, but this is met with skepticism; *if this was really happening, why didn't we know about it?* On the other hand, the principal who communicated proactively and told the story of a healthy, caring, and safe school will find allies in the community. The angry parent may begin to understand they didn't see the full picture.

"If you aren't telling your school's story, someone is telling it for you."

As our friends, Tony Sinanis and Joe Sanfelippo say, "If you aren't telling your school's story, someone is telling it for you." Great principals use multiple communication avenues to make sure they are in charge of telling their school's story.

Great principals also understand that everything is a part of telling the story: the curriculum, the policies, the programs, the staff, and the physical appearance of the facility. They also know that their story is communicated in every single message from the school. If you say your school is about students first, how is this shared? It needs to be shared not only in your own communications but also in the communications shared by teachers and students. Principled principals do not leave this to chance; they tell the school's story—consistently, clearly, and proactively.

Honest, Relevant, Timely, Varied

A school with effective communication systems has a multi-layered approach to sharing their stories. They likely use Twitter, Facebook, email, electronic and/or paper newsletters, and a host of other tools. Regardless of the tools they use, there are some common traits to all effective communication.

Honest

In the prior example about an upset parent, proactive communication only works if it is truthful. Not only is it unethical to tell a story of your school that is untrue, it is also ineffective. If you are not authentic in your communications, your teachers, parents, and students will quickly figure it out. The last thing you want to do is paint a picture of your school as something it is not. But at the same time, you can combine your desire to tell a positive story about your school with a call to action for making positive changes to affect a more positive school environment.

If you'd like your school to be known for supporting social emotional health, then communicate this sentiment, and ask for help in creating genuine action steps for students. If you would like your school to be known for stellar academic achievement, then communicate what needs to be done, why it matters, and how it can be accomplished together. Proactive communication means you share all the positive things you are doing as well as those things you intend to do as a school community.

We must also be honest when we communicate with parents about policies and procedures. Sometimes teachers and principals fear being honest because they are afraid the policy will make some people angry. Although our fears may be valid, these aspects are outside what Stephen Covey would call our "circle of control." We cannot control the reaction of the parent who was upset about their son being called a name. Furthermore, we cannot control their subsequent actions. What we can control is our own behavior. In that particular case, it meant being honest about what we learned about the incident, being honest that the incident was not bullying, and being honest that the matter had been dealt with appropriately. The parent may still be upset, and we may be upset as a result of the parent's reaction, but we take comfort in knowing we did our job and were 100 percent truthful every step of the way. It may not be rocket science, but great principals understand the importance of practicing what we teach our students every day: Honesty is the best policy.

Relevant and Timely

One of the misconceptions about effective communication is that, to do it effectively, we need to overdo it. We often hear people say you need to over-communicate with your stakeholders. Although we tend to agree with this statement in theory, we also believe the saying is often misinterpreted. Many people who hear this advice may think they need to send *more* actual communications: emails, newsletters, Tweets, or Facebook posts. In our view, over-communication is not about *quantity;* it's about *quality.*

When Anthony was a principal, he sent a single newsletter to families every week. He used Smore, an easy-to-use tool for designing online flyers and newsletters, to send an email called *Happy Friday, Kipling Families.* He embedded pictures and videos rather than just an email full of text. Because he only sent one per week, he wanted to make it as engaging as possible.

Not a week went by that a teacher or PTO member didn't ask Anthony to send a special email to all families in the school about something of great importance to the person making the request. These requests were especially frequent toward the beginning of the school year. The PTO wanted something sent about an ice cream social, a teacher wanted something special to be sent about school supplies, and the nurse wanted to tell parents about prescription medicine procedures. Although Anthony understood just how important this information was, he almost never sent any additional communications outside the weekly newsletter. His response was always, "I will be sure to include it in *Happy Friday, Kipling Families.*" This communication tool had become embedded into the school culture, and nearly all families turned to it first for the information they needed.

It is impossible to "over-communicate" in terms of quality, but it can be counterproductive to over-communicate in terms of quantity. We can send so many communications that some people will stop paying attention. There's a communication "sweet spot" when it comes to sending messages to our school community. In terms of regular communication, we have found that once each week is that sweet spot. Friday was the best day in our experience, as it allowed parents the weekend to read and process all the information as they prepared for the week ahead; in fact, the Smore program allowed Anthony to track the number of readers and hits on links within the newsletter. After a while, he noticed a pattern.

Initially, there were a large number of readers on Friday afternoon, but eventually, the numbers increased significantly on Saturday morning. It became routine for many parents to read the "Happy Friday" newsletter as part of their Saturday morning routine. On a weekly basis, there were over five hundred regular readers of this newsletter in a school with just over four hundred students.

The main reason the school newsletter was successful was because of the relevant content. But the regularity of the newsletter was nearly as important to its success. People like it when they know what to expect. Every Friday they were guaranteed to get a newsletter from the school with all the information they needed to know about the upcoming week and weeks ahead.

Great communication is about figuring out how to leverage your tools and resources to connect with your families and staff in meaningful ways.

Varied

Great communication is not a one-size-fits-all endeavor. As we suggested, sending a weekly newsletter to every family, every Friday, is effective, but does that have to be all they receive? Does the content of the newsletter need to be only words on a page? The answer to both of these questions is "Of course not." In today's world, there are numerous ways to communicate with our families, and excellent principals use a variety of means, including traditional techniques and social media tools, to share information and tell their schools' stories. Below are some tips and suggestions for using common social media and collaborative tools to enhance communication. Before you use these tools, it is crucial to have a written policy and clear administrative roles for postings—especially photos and video clips of students.

Facebook: This is the probably the social media tool that is guaranteed to reach your families. As of August 2017, Facebook had two billion monthly users. We are willing to bet that some of those two billion reside in your community. Create a school Facebook page that your parents, staff, and families can "like." Post pictures from events or great happenings at your school. Also post reminders about upcoming events. But remember—even when using Facebook—to monitor the *amount* of communication. Research has shown people are most engaged when a page posts between seven and ten times a week. Three posts is too few to maintain interest, and when we send more than ten, people begin to ignore posts. Sending too many posts can "crowd" Facebook user feeds and increase the likelihood that some will begin to assume the many messages are unimportant.

Twitter: Create a school Twitter account and a hashtag for your school. Get your teachers and families on Twitter. Have them post great happenings from your school, and include your school's hashtag in the Tweet. The hashtag acts as an identifier for the posts. Take it one step further and use Storify to catalog your school's Tweets from the week into a photo story using the school hashtag and send this out to families, including it in the weekly newsletter. This way families that are not on Twitter can still see it.

Hootsuite: Take your communication further, and save time by using a tool like Hootsuite to link your school's Twitter and Facebook accounts. Make one post through Hootsuite, schedule future posts, and choose if it goes to Facebook, Twitter, or both.

Seesaw: We love this innovative tool for schools. With Seesaw, students can create digital portfolios complete with photos, audio recordings, and videos. They can even upload documents. Parents can download the Seesaw app on their smartphone and link to their child and child's classroom. Parents receive a push notification when their child posts something. Through this app, parents can then go and "like" their child's post and/or comment on it.

Imagine a first grader posting a recording of themselves reading a book. At work, the parent receives a notification and is able to view and comment, "Great job! I am so proud of you!" The child receives this feedback immediately.

Teachers and principals also have this power. As a principal, Anthony made it a regular practice to comment and like posts students at his school uploaded into Seesaw. Kids loved it and always knew the principal took an interest in their learning.

Teacher Communication

As important as communication from the principal is, particularly about the school as a whole, the classroom teacher will always provide the most important and relevant communication to students and their families. Even the best principal-communicators cannot make up for a building with poor teacher-communicators. Let's assume all teachers regularly communicate with students and parents about the classroom, homework, and other items but miss a crucial aspect: communicating solutions rather than problems. Great principals lead their teachers in creating solution-focused communications rather than problem-focused communications.

Whenever a teacher contacts a parent about a concern with a child, the problem is almost always clear. But what is often lacking is a solution to the problem. Whenever teachers speak or write to parents about a concern with their child, those teachers should also include the steps they are taking to solve the problem. Too often, messages home to families look something like this:

> Dear Mr. and Mrs. Jones,
>
> I have noticed that Johnny has not been doing well lately in math. He does not seem to know his math facts and is not where he should be in terms of computation skills for this time of year. It would help Johnny to practice these at home.
>
> Thanks,
>
> Mr. Your Problem

If Johnny is struggling, there is absolutely no problem in conveying this information to Johnny and his parents. The teacher should; it's a teacher's responsibility, yet a teacher also has the responsibility to actually *help* Johnny. A parent who receives a message like this is left with nothing but concern and no clear way to deal with the problem other than to practice at home, taking on the responsibility for closing a learning gap. Messages like the one above heighten parent anxiety without resolving the problem.

A better and more appropriate message would be something along the lines of the following:

> Dear Mr. and Mrs. Jones,
>
> I have noticed that Johnny has not been doing well lately in math. He does not seem to know his math facts and is not where he should be in terms of math computation skills for this time of year. We are working to remedy this immediately. I have spoken to Johnny, and we came up with a plan to spend ten minutes a day at school reviewing and practicing his facts. I think it would help Johnny if you were involved too. Please talk to him nightly about what he is learning and review the facts we did with him

during the day. (He will bring home a sheet with that info.) I will keep you updated on his progress. I know he can get these mastered very quickly with a bit more practice and our support.

Thanks,

Mr. We're in This Together

Notice the difference between these two messages. One is problem focused and one is solution focused. If you can influence one practice regarding teacher communication in your school, make it this: Move your teachers from problem-focused communications to solution-focused communications. You will quickly see trust in your teachers rise to new levels as parents see teachers are focused on outcomes rather than just calling out problems.

Paper Cuts

A few months ago, a friend called us about an issue at his child's school. He wondered why the school sent home so much "stinking" paper. His child brought home nearly twenty pieces of paper daily. Some of it included the child's homework and other class assignments, but most of it was individual leaflet announcements about a PTO meeting, a movie night, a special lunch on Friday, and so on. Exasperated, he exclaimed, "I just can't keep up!" He had missed important events because sometimes the announcements got lost in the daily pile of flyers. "Why," he asked, "in today's world, do schools still communicate like this?"

Many schools do not communicate this way. But we also know that too many of our schools still do. Principals and schools need to get up to date in the digital age in terms of how we communicate and how much paper we send home. We advocate for this not just because it is easier for principals; it is also better for parents. Recent statistics reveal that 88 percent of people in the United States have access to the internet, and 77 percent have smartphones. Lack of internet access is no longer an excuse for not communicating digitally. Even in many communities with lower socioeconomic resources, internet access is still widely available. We must take advantage of this, making sure, of course, that we accommodate for families without access.

Think about how many people constantly check their phones for news or sports updates. Why not add updates from their child's school to the mix? Create an online email newsletter that captures all the announcements for your school, and have your teachers do the same for their classrooms. It will greatly reduce your parents' stress and will save lots of trees. Great principals overcommunicate, focusing on the quality, not the quantity, of their communications and try to limit the amount of paper they send home.

The Communication Principle

3-2-1

3

PRINCIPALS' PERSPECTIVES ON THE COMMUNICATION PRINCIPLE

Brad Gustafson (@GustafsonBrad) is Minnesota's 2016 Principal of the Year and the author of *Renegade Leadership*. He was recently named a National School Boards Association "20 to Watch" educator. He shares the belief that schools should be spaces where relationships, creativity, and innovation thrive. Brad knows the importance of modeling effective communication for those he leads and shares three specific characteristics he hopes to model when communicating:

When I'm communicating with our team and school community, I try to model the very same things I expect to see in our classrooms. In doing so, I try to communicate in a manner that models three characteristics:
1. Aligns to our vision (e.g., personalized learning)
2. Amplifies student voice
3. Creates dialogue, trust, and transparency

We personalize weekly email communication by sharing a link to an audio version of the very same email. This models "choice" for staff who may prefer to listen to a weekly communication while commuting or multi-tasking at their desk. It also allows me to lend my voice to content so that our team can literally hear my tone and concern for what's being communicated.

We integrate student voice and perspective into parent communications by creating podcasts with students. The podcasts have taken the place of lengthier principal newsletters and are created over the lunch hour with students. This transformative practice has allowed me to build deeper relationships with students while modeling digital leadership for them and others.

We're using social media to add additional transparency and authenticity to our communication. Instead of simply sharing out major projects once a month, we share smaller moments and day-to-day learning breakthroughs. We invite our staff and community to post these learning highlights to a school hashtag (#GWgreats). We added flat screen television sets to our office and entryway so everyone can view these important moments as they're happening. This practice has created a space where social media is used as "learning media," and dialogue is centered around the incredible work our students create.

We front-load certain meetings with video to enhance collaboration when we're together in person; for example, our "Flipped Open House" videos communicate short greetings, routines, and curriculum information from teachers prior to Open House. This way when we meet at the actual Open House, our focus is on building relationships and making students feel welcome. We use this same approach to "Flip School Board Meetings." (Of course, student voice is prominent in many of these videos!)

Michael Hobin (@mjhobin) is principal of Coventry High School in Rhode Island. He began his administrative career as an assistant principal in 2002 at Coventry High School where he taught physics education. In 2006, he became the eleventh principal in twelve years and has remained in the position for the past eleven years. In 2007, he was named the Outstanding First-Year Principal, and in 2013 Michael was named the High School Principal of the Year from the Rhode Island Association of School Principals. He knows the importance of clear, consistent, positive communications and shares a few of his strategies for achieving that at his school:

> How a principal communicates with the school community shapes the way all stakeholders perceive you. Today, teachers, students, parents, and community members expect to be informed on a timely basis by way of a variety of social media platforms. When effective communication is provided, principals gain the confidence of the many stakeholders that comprise the educational community.
>
> One of my first decisions as principal was to eliminate paper correspondence within the building and move strictly to email. Today I utilize Facebook, Twitter, Instagram, Snapchat, listserv, text messaging, Voxer, and screencasts. I also communicate with students by mailing "positive" postcards and note cards. And yes, I still utilize the personalization of a phone call. This personalization is especially appreciated when students and families are in crisis and have experienced a significant achievement.
>
> When I became principal, I was the eleventh principal in twelve years at our high school. With so much administrative turnover, I knew the high school had a culture and leadership problem to address. It was at this point that I read *Improving Your School, One Week at a Time* by Dr. Jeffrey Zoul. After reading this book, I committed to implement a "Friday Focus" for the staff. Friday Focus memos became my way of shaping school culture, offering intellectual discourse, and exploring instructional strategies to improve teaching and learning. Teachers responded positively to the Friday Focus, and together we began, one week at a time, to improve the school environment.

Since 2006 I have faithfully written to staff each week using a professional text as a source for learning. Several years ago, after reading *What Great Teachers Do Differently* by Todd Whitaker, I began highlighting a member of the school community who was observed contributing "just a little bit more" during the previous week. Their efforts were highlighted as the "Greatness of the Week" at the end of the Friday Focus. I believe this positive reinforcement has created a culture of excellence and kindness in the building. Additionally, during the 2016–2017 school year, I began to film a Sunday night screencast, primarily to promote the activities for the upcoming week. Many teachers have commentated that they have appreciated my commitment to exploring an educational text with them, highlighting staff accomplishments, and sharing important upcoming events with them.

I have found it helpful to have one branded "handle" for all media platforms: @coventryoakers. During my tenure, the social media platforms have changed. Parents are on Facebook and Twitter. Students love Instagram and SnapChat. Of course, listservs work well when an email message is needed. I have adapted to providing information for the school's stakeholders in formats each group utilizes most frequently.

Your school community deserves effective communication from its leader. If not you, whom? If not now, when? Regardless of what technological methods a principal selects to communicate with a school community, I encourage the messages to be direct, timely, and uplifting. Constantly reinforce your vision for the staff and students, and highlight the positives of the school's mission. Utilizing various communication platforms creates a positive school climate, enhances ways to personalize for the various school constituencies, and creates constructive dialogue.

Kristen Paul (@MrsKristenPaul) is a middle school principal in Barrington, Illinois. Prior to becoming a principal, Kristen spent three years as the Associate Principal in Deerfield, Illinois.

As a leader, Kristen constantly models how to use social media to shape the story of Barrington Middle School Station Campus by using platforms such as Twitter, Facebook, Edublog, and the website Smore. Kristen encourages teachers to explore what it means to be a connected educator and use the power of digital collaboration. Kristen is passionate about using social media as a communication tool for her school community and shares why this matters and how she uses such tools to share her school's story:

> Four years ago, when I heard the phrase "social media and educa-
> tion," I was perplexed, even though I was an active user (person-
> ally) of Facebook and Instagram. When it was suggested that I also
> explore using Twitter as an educator to tell the story of my students
> and staff, I did not know what this could possibly look like. With
> the encouragement of my mentor and colleague, I plunged into
> Twitter!
>
> I was pleasantly surprised to learn how easy it was to "Tweet"
> pictures of what staff and students were doing during their day
> as well as follow our school hashtag "#engage109." I also learned
> about different Twitter chats and groups such as the #apchat and
> #momsasprincipals. I found that connecting with other educators
> around the country not only increased my Professional Learning
> Network (PLN), but also provided me with so many more ideas of
> how to engage and inspire both students and staff.
>
> As a first-year principal, it is important to me that I model what
> it means to tell our story to our community. At the beginning of
> the year, I challenged staff members to #tellyourstory. I even had
> T-shirts made with this reminder! I want educators to not only con-
> nect with students individually by sharing their stories of who they
> are but to also model for students what it looks like to tell others
> who they are by using our school Twitter account (@StationMS220)
> and school Facebook page (Barrington Middle School Station
> Campus). With so many students using popular social media

platforms like Snapchat, it is important to me that teachers recognize students are already telling their story on a continual basis. In order for teachers and staff to "speak" the language of students, there needs to be a shift in the classroom narrative. Together we are exploring how to share our story as a school community by creating a school hashtag and also sharing our story using the popular social media platform TweetBeam.

As Tony Sinanis and Joseph Sanfelippo share in their book *The Power of Branding: Telling your School's Story*, it is important for school leaders to control the narrative about the "who" and "what" of their schools. As they suggest, if you do not control the narrative of your school, someone else will. I often encourage staff members with this reminder to take the opportunity to share all the great things they and their students are doing on a daily, weekly, and monthly basis with our school community. When others hear our school name, I want the questions to be not only "What is happening at that middle school?" but also "How can I learn from their story?"

2

COMMUNICATION PRINCIPLE RESOURCES

For a list of these and other resources, please visit theprincipledprincipal.com.

"Top 10 List for Successful Communications" and **"Communication Tips for Teachers"**

These are two excellent documents created by the Pattonville School District in St. Ann, Missouri, related to school communication. The former is geared toward principals, while the latter is aimed at teachers. We like the simple, clear, numbered, succinct format of these documents which reiterate several points mentioned in this chapter.

The Colorful Principal

This is the blog of Ben Gilpin, an elementary school principal in Michigan. Ben is an excellent principal who is a master communicator. He uses Twitter, Facebook, and various podcasting tools to spread his messages. In addition, he uses his blog site, The Colorful Principal, to post a weekly message that he shares with his school community and with the entire world through Twitter. Ben's weekly blog posts always include his thoughts on different aspects of education, what is happening at his school, and links to various video clips of interest and value to educators.

1

COMMUNICATION PRINCIPLE CULTURE CRUSHER

When staff members do not understand the "why" of decisions made in their school, we are destroying the culture of that school. Principled principals know the importance of communicating why they are doing what they do and why the school and/or district is implementing a new program, changing one that currently exists, or scrapping one altogether.

When staff members do not understand why something is happening, they are not only less likely to support it but also more likely to feel frustrated, confused, and even bitter. Such feelings among educators in a school crush the culture. Even the most collaborative school leaders know many decisions ultimately fall on them to make. When making such decisions, these principals also realize they cannot, and should not, please everybody. The same decision that makes many staff members happy may upset many others. Great principals seek input from all staff by listening to all perspectives and ensuring that everyone's voice is heard before making decisions that will impact the school.

Once the decision is made, they explain how the decision-making process worked and why the final decision was made. In schools led by great principals, not all staff will agree with all decisions made by the principal. But they will know *how* the decision-making process works and *why* a decision was made.

PRINCIPLE 8
The Management Principle

Management is doing things right; leadership is doing the right things.

—Peter Drucker

Are you a dreamer or a doer? Think about this question for a moment.

Dreamers see the future. They are visionaries who can imagine a better future for staff, students, and the entire school community. They are focused on the next marker on the horizon and are ambitious in making plans to get there. On the other hand, doers are roll-up-their-sleeves types. They are focused on the task at hand and get things done.

As opposite as dreamers and doers may seem from a cursory glance, the truth is that schools need principals who possess the qualities of both. It is great to have fantastic plans for the future, but to actually attain a better reality, it takes a lot of hard work and focus on every detail along the way. The management principle is all about how great principals take the visions and dreams they and others have for their schools and put the structures and systems in place that make them a reality.

In recent years, it seems that any discussion about school principals has centered almost entirely on principal "leadership," with very little space devoted to the idea of "management." We would even say the idea of management has become a bit taboo, not only in educational leadership literature but throughout all industries. Leadership may strike us as more flashy, bold, important, and future focused. But make no mistake: Just as schools will not become great without great leadership, they also will not become great without great management.

Who Owns What?

Management includes the day-to-day work of our schools, right down to the small details. One principal we know calls these the "blocking and tackling" aspects of his job. In football, blocking and tackling seldom receive the appreciation they deserve; instead, the glory tends to go to the quarterbacks, running backs, and wide receivers of the world. Of course, these passes, runs, and catches would never occur if not for the work of the less glamorous, but crucial, work of linemen.

Principled principals remember to focus on not only the more glamorous aspects of the job but also the "blocking and tackling." Who is responsible for what? Who orders those supplies? What is the agenda for the meeting? Whom do you call if the boiler goes down? What happens during a severe weather situation? How do the bus and car rider lines work? Excellent principals make sure everyone involved knows the answers to these and other management questions.

Great principals are visionary leaders who are also organized managers. They know the ins and outs of their buildings like no one else. They know whom to call if a problem or issue arises beyond the school's circle of control. They are adept at prioritizing everything from building schedules to team meetings to parent conferences. They understand the real fuel that moves them forward as a school is generated in the day-to-day work of everyone in the building.

Great principals are visionary leaders who are also organized managers.

Although it may not get a lot of attention, we maintain that people want strong management skills in their leader and want to work in a well-managed school. It has become fashionable to think that people disdain management, but what people really don't like is *poor* management. People like *good* management because it supports them and allows them to focus on the things that are most important as educators, knowing there will be no surprises from an operational standpoint.

One of the things Chicago is famous for is its long, cold, and windy winters. So it comes as no surprise that a fair amount of recess sessions during these months teeters on the edge of kids having to stay inside because it's too cold. During Anthony's first year as principal, as the weather grew colder, there was lively debate in the office about whether to stay inside for recess or go outside. The time-bound nature of the decision intensified the stress in the office. The office administrative assistants would discuss the situation with teachers and lunch supervisors. If a parent was in the office, they might weigh in too. The ultimate decision seemed to be made somewhat randomly. Sometimes it would be ten degrees outside, but sunny, so people thought it was okay. Other times, it would be twenty degrees outside, and they would want to keep the students inside because it was cloudy.

After some investigating, Anthony discovered a provision in the teachers' contract that said they would not be required to work outside if the temperature with wind chill fell to fifteen degrees or below. Of course, not everyone at the school who supervised recess worked under the teachers' contract guidelines, but this metric seemed reasonable for everyone. As a result, they decided that every day throughout the winter, the office would use the exact same weather website to determine the temperature, taking into account the wind-chill factor. At sixteen degrees or above, students went outside. If it was fifteen degrees or below, they stayed inside.

It's hard to believe, but such a simple management decision saved twenty minutes a day of debate. People who had sometimes walked away angry because the decision hadn't gone their way stopped giving this any thought whatsoever. We realize this is a simple example of a management issue, but, as principals, we are faced with hundreds of similar issues each school year. Effective principals invest no more time than necessary planning for these relatively minor management issues, but they *do* plan for them. When students should or should not go outside for recess is not a policy that should be subjective. The school had a metric to use. All that was needed was for someone to apply it.

Once this decision was finally enacted, there was no argument or push back from teachers and staff for two reasons: 1) It was absolutely clear why the decision was being made, since there was already a metric to apply, and 2) It took the debate off staff members' radars. When principals manage facilities, resources, and personnel well, they take mundane decisions off the plates of staff members. This, in turn, allows everyone to focus on the most important work they do: teaching and learning.

Another understanding great principals have is the importance of appropriate and productive collaboration. Great principals are collaborative leaders who utilize shared decision-making in their schools to achieve goals; however, this does not mean that everything needs to be a collaborative discussion. We often see principals make the mistake of thinking every single thing in a school needs to be decided by committee. Great principals understand there is a difference between decisions that should be made collaboratively and decisions that are straightforward administrative responsibilities.

> ## There is a difference between decisions that should be made collaboratively and decisions that are straightforward administrative responsibilities.

When students should go outside for recess is an administrative decision. Great principals do not cede the power of their administrative decision to the collective group. It benefits no one when they involve others in such decisions. Other examples of administrative responsibilities could be creating building schedules, room assignments, or class placements. In too many schools, these decisions are ceded to the will of the group. This becomes problematic when the will of the group is not in line with the best interests of the entire school.

Another elementary school principal we know is a master scheduler. When she became a principal at a new school, one of the first items on her to-do list was the master building schedule. For this principal, it was important for teachers to have a common time to plan and work together. Over the summer, when she first looked at the master schedule for the building (which dictated when certain classes went to subjects like art, music, or PE and when teachers had plan times), it struck her as rather haphazard. Decoding the master schedule was like trying to solve a Sudoku puzzle. When she inquired as to how the schedule was created, she learned the responsibility for creating it had been ceded from the principal to a small group of teachers. Now it began to make sense. The schedule was a compilation of various individual preferences for when teachers would have breaks. It did not, unfortunately, operate under principles of best practice, such as common planning time—even though that was what teachers collectively said they wanted.

So our friend started from scratch. She built the master schedule with an eye toward common planning time for teachers and balance for students. Ultimately she created a schedule that allowed teachers in a grade level to have at least thirty (and usually sixty) minutes of daily common planning time. The new schedule was well received by staff, as it was what the majority of teachers wanted. What the process was missing was someone to look at the schedule in an unbiased way with an administrative lens and an eye toward common school goals. This is a unique and valuable perspective that effective principals bring to situations, and it is why management issues like this should typically not be decided by committee.

Of course, the schedule was not set in stone once the principal created it. She communicated it to the entire staff, solicited feedback, and made changes based on this input. But everyone knew the overall goals of the schedule and the structures used to accomplish the goals, so it helped them to consider it from a broader perspective.

Like every effective school leader we know, we genuinely value the concept of authentic collaboration on any number of issues in schools. Two heads are almost always better than one, and three are typically better than two. Yet we must not waste the time of staff members by involving them in every decision—in particular, those that can be made soundly, swiftly, and objectively by the principal. Unfortunately, counterproductive shared decision-making occurs too often, particularly with new administrators. Sometimes we cringe when we ask people how they are going to solve a certain problem, and they respond along the lines of "I was thinking about forming a committee." This is not necessarily a bad way of thinking, but we must know when to apply it and when not to. Great principals understand the difference between decisions that should be made collaboratively and when they need to exercise more authority regarding specific systems and procedures relating to how the school is "managed."

Managing Up

One skill of great principals is their habit of "managing up." This simply means working with the superintendent, central office administration, school board, or other leaders in a productive and collaborative fashion. Again, the phrase is practically taboo at this point, but serving as a principal is a prime example of a "middle management" position. Principals are the filter between the central office and teachers at the school. As such, the relationship between principals and their colleagues serving in the central office must be based on trust and honesty.

One of the ways great principals "manage up" is to be completely clear about what is expected of them as a leader and manager. They ask questions to clarify and understand what roles the district leadership needs them to play. Principals should not be afraid to ask their superintendent questions such as "Why did you hire me?" and "What do you consider to be the most important aspects of my job?" Such questions help to clarify expectations the board and central office leaders have for principals. It also forces district leadership team members to think about these questions and be clear about what their specific expectations actually are. Great principals are not shy about reaching out regularly to their superintendent and others to learn if and when priorities and expectations change.

Principals also "manage up" by proposing solutions for their school or the district to the superintendent. When they reach out to the central office, it is not always to ask for help with a problem; they also reach out to identify solutions to problems and volunteer to help lead district-wide initiatives.

Great principals manage up effectively by knowing when to reach out for help, when to reach out to assist, and which problems to handle at the school level versus seeking input from leaders outside their own school. Great principals understand the chain of command, and they want to handle as many questions as they can without sending them to someone else. When we served as principals, our goal was to address concerns and answer questions ourselves, regardless of the topic; however, even though we always strove to solve problems at the building level, we also knew it was sometimes necessary to direct people to the central office or reach out to the central office about a particular issue. Great principals embrace the responsibility of managing their own crises but are also not afraid to reach out for help; knowing the difference between the two is a key trait of an effective manager. When a superintendent or assistant superintendent continually receives inquiries that should be easily handled at the building, it muddies the waters in the chain of command and can lead to confusion about responsibilities. At the same time, when central office leaders learn about an important situation that occurred at the school level from someone other than the principal, or only after it is too late to offer help, the principal has not done a good job of keeping others involved. Principled principals possess an uncanny knack for knowing when to make the central office aware of a situation, when to ask the central office for help in managing a situation, and when to reach out to the central office to offer support on issues that affect the entire district.

Managing Down

Another aspect of management is "managing down," not necessarily in a hierarchal sense in which we play the "boss" card, but in the way we collaborate, as appropriate, with teachers and other school personnel about school management matters. At times, successful principals must tackle management issues alone. There are other instances when it behooves them to do so in collaboration with invested staff members. And there are still other instances when the best course of action as a leader is to manage the situation, role, or responsibility by empowering some other staff member with the passion and expertise to manage specific aspects of the school's day-to-day expectations and procedures. Regardless of which role we assume in managing any school routine, the first key to effectively managing down is being crystal clear about our expectations. We must avoid ambiguity when outlining responsibilities for staff and teachers and cannot assume that people know what we are thinking. Individuals are much more likely to follow procedures if they are clear about what is expected of them. Whether great principals tackle school management issues alone, in collaboration with teacher leaders, or by empowering another staff member to manage the issue, they make sure everyone is clear about expectations.

Individuals are much more likely to follow procedures if they are clear about what is expected of them.

A second key to success in managing down is providing clear and timely feedback. One of a principal's major managerial responsibilities is the evaluation of teachers and other staff members. The evaluation process can be a difficult, time-consuming, and laborious part of our job. Although it is never a simple task, it can be made easier and more productive by always providing clear, direct, honest, specific, and constructive feedback. Great principals also understand the evaluation process can be stressful for many teachers. Although rarely the case, some teachers feel like their worth, performance, and maybe even future employment is on the line during the evaluation process. Principals must keep this in mind and control what they can about the process. This includes not only being clear about our expectations throughout the process, but also clear in our feedback. When teachers communicate with parents about their children, we do not want them to stop at simply identifying the learning or behavior problem; we want them to provide actionable solutions. The same holds true in this instance for principals. If we are going to provide critical feedback on a teacher's performance, we must go beyond merely identifying the problem. We must provide suggestions for improvement and help support teachers.

A key aspect in managing down is creating a culture of "yes" in your school. As principals, we do not have all the great ideas, nor can we be everywhere. We must empower others to lead and manage as well. A key to doing this is adopting the habit of saying, "Yes!" to people when they want to try something new. The only way we can encourage innovation in our schools is to create a culture that is open to new things. Great principals find ways to say yes to ideas, innovation, and risk taking, empowering people to succeed and making the school better. They do not micromanage all aspects of school initiatives, but they do keep an eye on the ever-important outcomes of each initiative.

The Management Principle
3-2-1

3

PRINCIPALS' PERSPECTIVES ON THE MANAGEMENT PRINCIPLE

Jennifer Frantz (@Jenn_Frantz) is principal of the Lower Elementary School in the New Hope-Solebury School District in Bucks County, PA. This is her fourteenth year in education. She spent eleven years teaching elementary school in the Central Bucks School District and two years as the assistant principal in the Centennial School District, both in Bucks County. She is a true advocate for students and values collaboration, risk taking, and the art of being reflective. Jenn knows the importance of ensuring the school runs well from a management and operations standpoint; she also knows that by sharing management responsibilities, she is empowering others to lead:

> Management. It's not shiny, but it is a necessary component of leading a successful building. As the principal of any building, large or small, keeping the ship afloat requires constant check-ins with the "nuts and bolts" of your organization. Managing all your clients—teachers, parents, support staff, community members, and most importantly, students—can raise the anxiety level of even the most seasoned principal. For me, as a new principal, it can seem especially daunting. How do I balance management with leadership? I am certainly not the first person to ask this question.

In the spirit of taking my new leadership position one step at a time, my goal is to make management decisions with a leader's eye. In creating my building's schedule, I look to make it as student centered as possible, with respect to the educators on the front lines. I schedule monthly meetings with my secretary (a true saving grace) so we can look ahead and see what we need to start preparing for so as not to be overwhelmed at the last minute.

And lists. Oh, the lists. I make them. I re-make them. I get immense pleasure out of crossing items off as they are wrapped up by the end of the day, week, and month. I talk to people. I learn their strengths. This allows me to empower others to create and complete projects. By distributing the management, I am also distributing the leadership. I am building a culture where the smartest person in the room is . . . the room.

Managing a building isn't glossy. It requires forethought, organization, and grit. But it is also leadership in wolf's clothing. When done in the right spirit, managing a successful school can also grow true leaders from within its own walls.

Brian McCann (@casehighprinc) is principal at Joseph Case High School in Swansea, Massachusetts. A graduate of Boston College and The University of Michigan, Brian was named Massachusetts' 2011 High School Principal of the Year and most recently presented on school culture at ISTE and the National Principals Conference. As a veteran school leader, Brian knows he has a lot to do, but he cannot do it alone. He shares his perspectives on empowering others and relying on others to help him lead and manage the school:

School management is more about people than crisis control. I am now in my fourteenth year of leading the high school from which I graduated, and I must admit this epiphany took its time in dawning on me. At first, I focused on making everyone happy and taking on way too much that should have been delegated to others. As a building leader, you cannot possibly "do" everything, so you must hire great people while empowering existing faculty to augment your strengths. We must learn to be "doers" who do not have to "do it all."

As with many aspects of our profession, trust is key. Modeling your expectations is just as important. You must have a vision and communicate it effectively. Dreams are great for a school, but can they be realized? They can if we manage the day to day effectively while also keeping our eyes on the longer-term vision. I manage day to day by listening. I listen to the administrative assistants who prioritize my day while safeguarding against distractions. I listen to my assistant principal and empower him to make decisions. His quiet resolve complements my zeal for our school, and stakeholders benefit from our complementary styles. He is my sounding board and first "phone-a-friend." I listen to my go-to teachers who know the pulse of the school. They tell me when things are working and when I need to iterate.

School principals need to catch up and manage their schools digitally. Leaders need to take control of the stories that are told, especially in different social media venues. So many from my Twitter-based PLN advise that schools must tell their stories before someone else does. By being proactive in celebrating your school via social media, school culture is strengthened by establishing new bonds with parents and families.

Finally, it is good for leaders-as-managers to understand the mechanics of their facility, but it's even better to really know their students and teachers. Without personal bonds of trust, no risk taking or magic can happen. At our school, we begin each year by prioritizing relationship building in the #1st3days and then build upon this strong base for the next 177 days.

I love serving as a high school principal. My management style works well in my community because it is personal, empowering, and student focused. When leaders prioritize people, we can accomplish great things.

Dave Ferguson (@RHS_VAprincipal) is the principal at Rappahannock High School in Warsaw, Virginia. Dave previously served as Richmond County's Director of Special Education for one year and as an assistant principal for six years. Prior to his administrative experiences, Dave taught special education for five years at Rappahannock High School. To serve successfully as a high school principal and manage the many aspects that come with the position, Dave knows he must rely on others within the school to help lead the way:

> The great part, and the hardest part, about education and being a school leader is that no single day is ever the same. Knowing this, how do we get things done and manage our school? Not knowing what is going to happen from one day to the next can create some concern when managing a school, but if you trust in your team, it will be okay. I think one of the most important things to keep in mind when managing or coaching in your school is that it is okay not to know the answer to everything and to allow others to lead and make decisions.
>
> I always cringe when I hear the phrase, "Well, that's why you make the big bucks." I am entering my third year as a building principal, and I may have ideas and experiences, but I do not know everything. I have to trust our faculty and staff to help our school and allow them the opportunities to lead in our classes, departments, and school community on a daily basis. Management is not always about your ideas and beliefs moving forward; it is about having the confidence in the team to make split-second decisions. I sing their praises and help them realize we all make mistakes when leading, but that's part of the learning process, just like our students' experience in the classroom.
>
> When you trust and empower your faculty and staff to make decisions based on the climate and culture you have created, things can be done in a timely fashion. You'll also create leaders in your school while also making your day, as principal, more manageable.

As a manager of a school, we must remember the most important piece of our work is the relationships we form. The members of our work family are humans, not robots. Make sure you know your team members as family and not just as people with whom you work. It makes a big difference when your team knows you see them as more than just employees.

Finally, as a school leader, don't forget your own family. We spend so much time working with our school family that the people waiting for us at home do not always get the attention they need and deserve. This amazing calling of leading a school is our career, but at the end of the day, that job could be lost and we will still have our family there to love us and support us. It is important to find the balance between managing career and home responsibilities.

2

MANAGEMENT PRINCIPLE RESOURCES

For a list of these and other resources, please visit theprincipledprincipal.com.

"Management By Walking Around (MBWA): The Essential Guide"

The idea that effective managers are effective, in part, due to their high visibility throughout the organization has been around since the 1980s. Perhaps first popularized by Peters and Waterman in their seminal management book, *In Search of Excellence*, the idea that effective managers "walk around" their organizations regularly is still a practice in many companies, such as Apple, Disney, and Starbucks, whose founder, Howard Schultz, regularly visited Starbucks shops weekly. Effective school managers are also highly visible, present in classrooms, cafeterias, at school functions, in the bus line, and during recess. Principals who actually see what is going on in all aspects of the school are better equipped to manage the school. This article focuses on business leaders and the MBWA practice but is equally applicable to school leaders.

"The Omnipresent Principal"

In this short post, Paul Young offers eleven tips for serving as an "omnipresent" principal to stay connected with everyone in the school community and all aspects of the school's operations.

1

MANAGEMENT PRINCIPLE
CULTURE CRUSHER

In life, there are "good" surprises and "bad" surprises. In a school, more often than not, we want to avoid any surprises in terms of the day-to-day operations of the school. When there are too many unpleasant surprises in our school which alter the expectations of staff and/or students, we are destroying the culture of that school. Examples of this include a surprise, last-minute change to the daily schedule, a hastily called meeting, a canceled safety drill, or a critical performance review coming out of the blue. Effective principals work to minimize the number of these surprises throughout the school year.

Principled principals build the culture of the school by serving as meticulous planners and schedulers who double- and triple-check everything that is planned at the school on a monthly, weekly, and daily basis—making sure to send reminders, follow up on all planning for events, and communicate proactively about anything that might be a surprise to staff members. When they learn something will not be happening according to plan, they notify any affected person immediately, apologizing if appropriate, and explaining what happened, why it happened, and what will happen instead.

Great principals are organized planners who realize great teachers are also organized planners and respect this trait in others. As a result, they always work to build the culture by building the confidence in their colleagues regarding the effective and efficient management of all aspects of the school's operations.

PRINCIPLE 9
The Harmony Principle

Happiness is not a matter of intensity but of balance,
order, rhythm, and harmony.

—Thomas Merton

There are two coffee shops near Jeff's home, and he is a frequent customer. Which one he goes to largely depends on his route to work in the morning.

One of the establishments is meticulously maintained and organized with a friendly atmosphere—obvious from the interactions between employees and customers—and a system that accommodates all of those complex latte and frappuccino requests. He sincerely enjoys stopping in, knowing he will chat with the employees and other customers while waiting for his drink. When ready, he knows it will come with a "See ya later. Have a great one, Jeff!" As a result of the pleasant environment, even if there is a long wait, he doesn't really mind.

The other coffee shop, however, is disappointing . . . to put it mildly. Walking in, it feels disorganized and unwelcoming. Products on shelves are in disarray, small spills are not cleaned up immediately, employees rarely speak to each other—and when they do, they are often short or even rude. Placing an order there feels like a mere business transaction without any meaningful human interaction.

Jeff wondered what could make the experience in these two coffee shops so different. He happened to visit the not-so-great coffee shop when the manager was working, and the answer became quite clear. The manager that day was in full-on, five-alarm fire mode. They were out of caramel syrup, and some-one forgot to stock the spill stoppers. Jeff knows these details because it was announced to the entire shop. The manager was running back and forth behind the counter trying desperately to look like she was in charge, but she had no noticeable game plan. It was clear there was a problem in the coffee shop that morning and equally clear she was the only person who could solve it—at least that's what she wanted her employees and customers to think.

The leader's voice should never be the voice *raising* the level of stress and anxiety.

This experience reminds us of the principalship and leadership in general. Whether you serve as an assistant principal, a dean, or a superintendent, the leader's voice should never be the voice *raising* the level of stress and anxiety; rather, theirs should be the voice that *lowers* it.

Some people adhere to the faulty belief that strong leaders are people who discover a crisis and then run around yelling (like in *Braveheart*) to solve the problem. Sadly, leaders who behave this way often end up creating a crisis where one doesn't exist. A byproduct of this leadership "style" is an entire group of staff, parents, and students operating at heightened and unsustainable emotional states. This leads to negativity that begins to seep into all aspects of their own work.

All schools need to have a sense of urgency, particularly about student learning. The work we do is too important not to have a sense of urgency every day; however, there's a big difference between a "sense" of urgency and an actual emergency. Great principals understand one of the key aspects to their job is to create harmony, not chaos, throughout the environment. This is the foundation of the harmony principle for principals.

Keeping Things in Perspective

One of the most important things principals can do is to remind themselves—and others—daily how fortunate they are to work in the field of education. Whenever we walk into a kindergarten or first-grade classroom, we marvel at all the things students this young know and can do. When we visit high school classrooms, we are often struck by the rigorous work in which we see students engaged and the sincere fun teachers and students have interacting. Whether we are visiting elementary, middle, or high school classrooms, we are always reminded how lucky we are to work in jobs that allow us to spend our time with these young learners. We must never lose sight of the fact that we serve in the world's most noble profession. We work in some of the most joyous and inspirational environments imaginable. In fact, in 2015, *Forbes* magazine identified the job of school principal as the happiest across any industry. Like all educators, great principals experience stress, conflict, and an almost overwhelming amount of items on their to-do lists. The difference between these great principals and less successful ones is their ability to keep things in perspective.

There are some true emergencies that occur in schools, which require swift action from principals. We all know the news stories of violent intruders in buildings. A student injury or parental dispute that spills into the school can cause alarm. Incidents like these are very real, yet they are the exception in our lives as educators, not the norm. For the most part, on a daily basis, what can cause those working in schools a great deal of stress are simply everyday problems to be solved. A teacher's car broke down on the way to school, and there is no substitute teacher available. Two people booked the conference room at the same time. The internet goes down. A student forgot their Chromebook. None of these things are fun to deal with. But such problems should never result in the principal, or any other staff member, becoming upset or overwhelmed. The principal or designee simply needs to solve the problem and then move on to solve the next one. The most effective principals we know do this while smiling, reminding others that it is not the end of the world.

One way principals can keep things in perspective is to understand that problems will arise. When managing dozens (or hundreds) of staff members and hundreds, if not thousands, of students and parents, our goal should not be to never have a problem. That is unrealistic. Our goal should be to have systems and cultures in place that minimize the number and impact of such incidents. To let problems frustrate us because they occur is futile. Regardless of the systems we have in place or the amount of preparation we have done, there will always be a next issue to address or problem to solve. Accept this as part of our work and you, along with others in the school, will be much happier.

Stay Calm and Lead On

Great principals rarely, if ever, get caught up in situations perceived as emergencies—except those, of course, that are actual emergencies. What others perceive to be an emergency may, in fact, be nothing of the sort. A concerned staff member may approach the principal with something they view as a huge problem. What they need from us in that moment is not to validate their worst fears by matching their intensity; they need us to calmly put their problem into perspective. A classroom that is too hot or too cold or not having enough chairs at an assembly are not examples of emergencies. Great principals make sure people know the principal understands the difference between a real emergency and a perceived one. If we match frustration and intensity with frustration and intensity, who is going to be there to help calm *us* down?

> **If we match frustration and intensity with frustration and intensity, who is going to be there to help calm *us* down?**

All organizations include some team members who seem to thrive on creating crises. Schools are no exception. These individuals enjoy being in a constant state of crisis, and they want you and the entire school to be there with them. They have an almost supernatural ability to transfer their fears to an entire grade-level team, staff, families, and—most damaging of all—students.

You know who these people are, and the rest of your staff does too. These are the staff members who always find a problem, no matter the issue. They begin nearly every sentence with "Well, I just don't know what we're going to do about blah, blah, blah . . . " You could give these people ten thousand dollars to decorate their classroom, and they'd complain about how stressful it was to figure out what to buy. Go out of your way to give these people the maximum strength calm-down treatment; the moment you match this person's urgency, you are playing a game you cannot win against an opponent with years of experience. Make sure the person raising the stress level of others is never you. Great principals are constantly monitoring themselves to ensure they are in harmony with their surroundings and modeling the harmony principle for others.

Stay Calm and Lean On

One of the most serious mistakes we see principals make is not asking for help when they need it. Not reaching out when you need help is a sign of weak leadership, not strong leadership. Reaching out for help can take different forms, from contacting fellow principals in the district, in another district, or through one's Twitter network. It may also include alerting central office personnel to the problem, but more often than not, great principals seek advice from leaders they respect to help them problem solve before turning an issue over to someone in the central office.

Just as the principal serves teachers so that teachers can better serve students, the superintendent, assistant superintendent, and other district office leaders exist to support principals in their role. Great principals are not afraid to lean on these fellow leaders for support. However, central office leaders are not the only people on whom they lean when faced with difficult situations or decisions; in fact, the best principals we know often lean on teachers within their own building for support. These principals know which teachers are true leaders who will always find time to provide honest, thoughtful, and calm advice. Even the calmest principals get stressed out at times. When they do, they are not afraid to turn to a trusted teacher to calm them down. Whether they turn to fellow principals, district office administrators, PLN members, or teachers in their own school, one way great principals *stay calm and lead on* is by leaning on others.

The Calmest Person in the Room

In times of stress, conflict, and crisis, the principal should be the calmest person in the room—working to reduce the anxiety of all involved, regardless of the participants. As principals, it is simply a fact that we're going to regularly encounter frustrated teachers, students, or parents. Keep in mind they want a problem to be solved, or, at a minimum, a problem to be *acknowledged*. It is nearly impossible to do either if your level of stress and anxiety is equally elevated. Maintaining balance in approaching and responding to such situations allows us to maintain harmony in our school. Great teachers know their students will largely model their own behavior off examples they set. The same holds true for principals. Principals who become visibly agitated, frustrated, and overwhelmed in front of others will likely find themselves with a staff full of easily agitated, frustrated, and overwhelmed teachers. On the other hand, a principal who always seems to be the calmest person in the room during times of conflict likely works with a growing number of teachers who are also calm, cool, and collected during difficult times.

Very few people want to work in a toxic environment. Most people, in fact, want to work in a harmonious environment. In schools, whether they serve in the former or latter is largely determined by the principal, the leader who sets the harmony tone. As leaders, we must always model emotional intelligence, leading and living in harmony with others. Our best people expect it, desire it, and deserve it. The only people who actually want us to lose our composure are the few miserable people who are looking for company. Principled principals behave in ways they want others to emulate, creating harmony in their schools.

The Management Principle
3-2-1

3

PRINCIPALS' PERSPECTIVES ON THE HARMONY PRINCIPLE

Sean Gaillard (@smgaillard) is principal at Lexington Middle School in Lexington, North Carolina. For the last twenty-five years, Sean has served as an educator in various roles including English teacher, assistant principal, and principal. In addition, Gaillard has written for *Education Week, Kahoot!,* and *Education Closet.* Sean's first book, *The Pepper Effect,* will be published in 2018. As a school leader, Sean exudes positivity and is able to spread joy and enthusiasm in the school he leads, and beyond:

"You are making it happen!" In the midst of the mania that comes with deadlines and demands in the schoolhouse, I find myself frequently sharing this statement with either a student, teacher, or family member. As a lead learner in my schoolhouse, I believe it is necessary to be a model of positivity, balance, and good.

Many have written about the rigorous demands that can hinder our momentum as principals. We face those challenges, and the beat goes on. Within the last few years, I shifted my paradigm as a principal to embrace and champion the positive. I was fatigued from outsider assumptions creating false realities of our schoolhouse. I wanted my teammates to tune in to what was right with our school, so I created the #CelebrateMonday hashtag to share the positive things happening at the beginning of each week. We tweeted out those many positives and experienced a positive shift in our school culture as a result. It really is that simple. Proclaiming the real goodness in our classrooms and highlighting those positives created a harmonious key in which we did indeed #TrendthePositive.

Although sharing those school positives via social media make an impact, it is important to take those 140-character moments to the next level. When I was in a band during my college days, we would also make the statement, "You are making it happen." In that context, it meant that a bandmate was in the musical zone and creating a joyful sound. It was a rallying cry for the rest of the band that we were heading in the right direction. I apply that same statement to our school. My daily and weekly blog for our faculty begins with "Praise and Thanks for Making It Happen." This is where I give positive shout-outs to various faculty members for making an intentional effort to make a difference. I also make "Praise and Thanks for Making It Happen" the first agenda item on any faculty meeting. Most importantly, the power of sharing those moments in person goes a long way in promoting harmony in a schoolhouse.

Harmony is the first key in which any school leader must play and resonate unabashedly in the schoolhouse. Schools are places where dreams are ignited and sustained. Those dreams have to be nurtured within a culture that is positive and inviting. The principal must lead the band in that key at all times in service and support of all students in the schoolhouse!

Michael Bostwick (@M_Bostwick) is an intermediate school principal in New York who is committed to providing authentic learning experiences fueled by igniting relentless passion in others. Michael has also served as a middle-level science teacher and STEM curriculum/professional developer. He has presented for the National Science Teachers Association at their national conference on the topic of Interactive Formative Assessment as well as at ISTE, speaking on Igniting a Culture of Innovation. Michael is a master at modeling harmony, especially during times of conflict:

One our greatest challenges as school leaders is to preserve harmony during arduous times. While this may seem exhaustingly impossible in the moment, handling these situations with care can actually strengthen your school culture in the long run. I have found that developing systems for clear and ongoing communication is critical, especially as we navigate through difficult situations. Clear, concise emails help to disseminate information, but I prefer face-to-face interactions whenever possible. I offer several "staff chats" strategically timed, based on the pulse of the building, which allow folks to ask questions, share concerns, or simply vent. I'd much rather offer this venue, winch allows productive dialogue and brainstorm potential solutions, than have a talk in the hallways that can drown us in negativity. I also like to keep my office door open as much as possible so I can serve as a resource to anyone who needs me at their convenience. In those conversations, we must be cognizant of our tones, body language, and words.

I vividly remember the time when one of my teachers walked into my office and dropped some devastating news. It took all she had to choke out the statement that her brother had just passed away unexpectedly. As a leader, I thought about how I could support and comfort her in her obvious despair. We need to be conscious of the energy and aura we emit, and I was sure to remain calm, express my sorrow, and comfort with genuine empathy. I later heard that my response to her grief made a difference in her moment of crisis.

The systems and culture we create serve as our "autopilot" in times of distress. That way when we need to fall back, we fall back on our clearly established vision and the "why" of our work. Our school culture is nothing short of a true family, and I believe that's a vital ingredient to maintaining harmony. We take care of each other through messy state mandates, house fires, deaths in our family, or whatever else is thrown our way. Our "why" is rooted in providing students with authentic learning experiences that are meaningful now and to their futures. Part of that recipe must undoubtedly contain the element of fun.

We celebrate Mondays to get students excited about returning to school rather than breaking the door down on Friday to get out. Our school has monthly spirit days with all staff and students wearing our school colors to demonstrate school pride. We have whole school assemblies called "Epic Events" with staff vs. student competitions like Family Feud or Minute to Win It. We also keep our "why" at the forefront by celebrating student and staff successes. I start every meeting with a five-minute discussion of recent celebrations, and after a busy day, that is the medicine that helps us forge forward.

We should be allowed to speak out with our own personal opinions, but we also need to unite with one voice. No voice is more important than those of our students. Our teachers not only allow for student voice and choice, but we encourage it through student leadership team, student-run classrooms, community building, student-developed classroom constitutions, and much more. Students then can become the glue that strongly binds us in difficult times and, most importantly, helps maintain harmony.

Lindsy Stumpenhorst (@lmstump) is principal at Washington Elementary School in Sterling, Illinois, a rural community two hours west of Chicago. As principal, Lindsy expects students and teachers to work hard, but she doesn't expect them to do it alone. Most days you will find her providing staff with learning-and-growing experiences in between games of soccer or tetherball with students at recess. Lindsy knows schools are filled with students and staff members who have busy lives and that, at times, emotions can become elevated. As a result, she models a balanced lifestyle, strives to be "present" in the moment, and works intentionally to exude an attitude of calm during times of crisis:

> I live on a farm, and when I take care of the animals, I put in my earbuds and let my playlist roll. On one particularly long chore day, I was blasting Katy Perry. I may have also been singing like I was on stage during the knockout rounds of *The Voice*. I didn't realize my husband and his friend had parked in the driveway just as I sang the infamous long high note on her hit "Dark Horse."
>
> As I wrapped up the lyric, I heard a voice behind me cheer, "Nailed it!" I spun around, saw the men grinning, and I knew they were an unintended audience to my performance. I was mortified!
>
> Being an elementary principal can feel like a ride on a "crazy horse." Everyone seems to need attention, and they need it right now. There is a delicate balance between giving time to everyone who needs it both at home and at school, and I've come to

understand this scale will hardly ever be even. Some days I give so much to school that my own family is an unfortunate afterthought. Other days, I am all in at home, and school never crosses my mind. In our school, I constantly remind myself that our students and staff are not unlike me in this regard, and I work to ensure that we keep this in mind during the calm as well as the inevitable not-so-calm moments in our school days. Emotions among students and staff can run high at times, and when they do, it is the job of school leaders to project a sense of calm to quell the chaos.

There is a natural ebb and flow to the demands between career and home, and I make a conscious effort to be aware of where I'm investing my attention. There is also an ebb and flow at school from calm times to moments of potential chaos. A primary role of the school principal is to realize these competing demands are inevitable and to remind everyone to keep things in perspective. One way I try to do that is to focus on the moment.

As an educational leader and as a person outside of school, I strive to give 100 percent to whomever I'm with in the moment. When I intentionally do this, I find I am better able to keep myself and others in harmony. Fortunately, I am much better at harmonizing the different aspects of my life than I am at my Katy Perry duet!

2

HARMONY PRINCIPLE RESOURCES

For a list of these and other resources,
please visit theprincipledprincipal.com.

"How to Stay Calm When You Know You'll Be Stressed"
In this TED Talk, neuroscientist Daniel Levitin, author of *The Organized Mind*, discusses how to stay calm and avoid making critical mistakes in stressful situations.

"10 Ideas to Help Teachers Beat Stress"
This article from *The Guardian* is full of tips from education experts on how to reduce teacher stress.

1

HARMONY PRINCIPLE
CULTURE CRUSHER

When we focus on petty issues in our school, we crush the culture of the school. When we allow others to act like these petty issues are real crises, we crush the culture. Although effective principals are always willing to listen to staff concerns, they are careful not to join in the frenzy of the moment; instead, they respond in ways to deflate the tension of the moment. Even when principals find that a situation is, in fact, a real emergency, they exude a sense of calm, modeling for others how we behave when things go awry.

Principled principals engage in intentional behaviors to "keep the calm" during stressful moments, including these five culture builders:

1. **Reframing**: They try to reframe what is happening for themselves and others. They recognize that anger or heightened emotions are natural responses to setbacks, and emotions can take over. As a result, they remind themselves that anger or frustration is normal as a first step in reframing the feelings people have.

2. **Context**: When working through the moment, they remind themselves and others to ask, "What's the worst thing that can happen as a result of this?" Often they will realize what seems like a big deal now won't be one later.

3. **Nonverbals**: They monitor non-verbals with intention, trying to keep the frown or scowl off their faces. If we look miserable, we generally will feel miserable, and this will rub off onto those we lead. Even in times of stress and escalated negative emotions, they smile as a way to calm others and themselves.

4. **Humor**: They know the importance of a healthy sense of humor about life and try not to take themselves—or momentary stressful events—too seriously.

5. **Positive Messaging**: Instead of constantly telling others they are overwhelmed or swamped, effective principals use more positive messaging, letting others know they, too, are busy, but that they will get through it and everything will be okay. "We have a lot going on right now, but we will get

through it all. We always do." Using more positive terms instead of negative ones as a daily intentional practice lessens the chances that others will erupt when things go wrong. They focus on the light at the end of the tunnel, not the tunnel itself.

PRINCIPLE 10
The Collaboration Principle

If everyone is moving forward together, then success
takes care of itself.

–Henry Ford

The concept of strong collaboration permeates every chapter of this book, but the topic merits its own chapter as perhaps the most important of the ten principles.

Almost as important as collaborating with all members of the school community is another type of collaboration: how the principal works as part of a shared leadership team with other principals and with their district office team.

All great principals understand their school is not an entity unto itself. Almost all schools are part of a larger district that consists of at least a few other schools, and every school in our nation is part of a larger network known as American education. Although school districts across our great nation can be alike in many ways, they also differ. Some districts are comprised entirely of elementary schools, while others are districts with only high schools. Others, of course, are consolidated or unit districts with all levels of schools from preschool to high school included. The makeup of school districts often varies widely depending upon the state in which one resides. The state of Virginia, for example, has just over one hundred school divisions or districts, while in Illinois that number is over eight hundred. In Illinois, some school "districts" are comprised of a single school, and in many of those cases, the principal of the lone school is also the superintendent of the district. Regardless of whether you are in a small or large district, the idea that any one school is part of a larger entity is important.

Great principals recognize the importance of their school's success *and* the importance of the district's success—aligning the mission and vision of the school with their district's mission and vision. We maintain that every school in the world is a unique community of teachers and learners with a unique system of traditions, stories, celebrations, myths, norms, beliefs, attitudes, and behaviors, all of which contribute to a unique school culture. And it is important that each school maintains its own identity. That identity, however, should be informed by, and in sync with, the mission, vision, values, and goals of the larger district.

When a new principal begins serving as a school leader, one of the most important things they can do is gain a clear understanding of what the overall district stands for and is striving for. Often these are incorporated into some sort of strategic planning document, an excellent starting point for a principal new to a district. Excellent principals make time to discuss with their superintendent how their school can advance the mission and vision of the entire district. Each school can take on its own persona, and all school leaders find unique ways to solve problems, but each school is also part of a vision of a larger community. Superintendents report to school boards and principals report to superintendents. Principals are directly linked to the larger mission and vision of the organization and community in which they serve. They, therefore, make it a point to collaborate with teachers, administrators, and even parents from across the district rather than merely within their own school.

> **Principals are directly linked to the larger mission and vision of the organization and community in which they serve.**

Stand Up

Effective principals sincerely value both student voice and teacher voice in their schools. They believe these voices matter and can make the school they serve much better. Great principals also value another voice: their own. Just as they ask students and staff to stand up and speak out about important matters at the school, they also make sure to stand up and be heard at the district level. Principled principals contribute to conversations respectfully, professionally, and *honestly*—even when their voice may be different from others on the team. Serving as a principal means you stand for something, have beliefs about student learning, and have values based on what is best for students, which you will not allow to be compromised. This means you have an obligation to speak up when you see decisions that would not be in the best interests of your students and, ultimately, the district.

Great principals advocate for their teachers, families, and, most importantly, their students. This doesn't just mean the school district personnel. It means at all times, with all people and organizations, including parent teacher organizations. One principal we know encountered a situation with a PTO that required her to stand up forcefully for one student in particular. While planning a holiday party for classrooms, the parent teacher organization was planning activities that involved food for holiday parties. The principal decided that because there were so many students with allergies in the school, the holiday party should not include food and should instead be centered around art, song, and game activities.

The parent teacher organization was not happy about this decision, as food had always been a traditional part of school holiday parties. PTO leaders even suggested a compromise to have the students with allergies leave the classroom during the holiday party. The principal stood firm and clearly explained to the PTO that she would not sacrifice the health, safety, and emotional well-being of any student so that other kids could eat candy, cake, and ice cream in their classroom. As she explained, parents of students with severe allergies send their kids to school with deep concern that something might happen to cause the child to have a reaction. The safety of students was this principal's top priority.

Surprisingly, this was not an easy situation for the principal, as she met stiff resistance from many in the parent community. Of course, parents of students with allergies were grateful, but their voices were a distinct minority. Despite the pushback, this principal stood firm for what she believed was best for all students and did not waver. Her commitment was to students, not to convenience or tradition. Eventually she was able to convince many parents to come around to the idea that the world would keep spinning if students did not eat candy, cake, and cookies in classrooms during holiday parties.

We would like to think that all principals would stand as firm, but we have known far too many cases in which others have caved to similar pressures. Being a principled principal means you stand for what's right for students at all times, not just when it is convenient. As a result of this principal's experience, she asked her superintendent if she could lead a district task force comprised of students, staff, and parents from across the district to study student food allergies and make a recommendation to the Board so all schools could adopt the same food guidelines. The superintendent was thrilled that she was willing to stand up and take the lead on this important issue and empowered her to lead the work. Just over one year later, the Board adopted a new, comprehensive food and allergy plan for all schools. By first taking a stand and then collaborating with her superintendent and others across the community, this outstanding principal helped make the entire district better.

Collaboration or Competition?

One of the things great principals recognize is the difference between collaboration and competition among colleagues within their school district. In schools with healthy school cultures, teachers are collaborative, not competitive. They *are* competitive when it comes to competing against *themselves* in that they are always trying to be better tomorrow than they were today.

When it comes to their fellow teachers, however, they are strong collaborators who take genuine joy in the success of their colleagues. The same holds true for principals and how they approach their work with fellow principals. Serving a school district as principal means serving as part of a collective leadership team. A true collaborative administrative team uses the successes of each member to improve as a team, with each individual principal using the success of others to improve themselves. The overwhelming majority of great principals check their egos at the door when approaching a collaborative venture of any kind involving the school district. Most also accept the fact that they are not geniuses but, instead, have succeeded through grit, perseverance, and the willingness to seek out new ideas.

Sadly, we know many principals who do not operate this way, and we suspect you know some too. These are the principals who do not want any other school to do better than their school because they fear it makes them look bad. They are the first to shoot down innovative ideas at their own schools and discourage new practices at other schools. They seem to take personal offense when a school is doing something they are not. These principals have their personal self-worth wrapped up in their schools, and in order to protect it, they are willing to stifle the success of others.

Great principals embrace the success of others.

Great principals embrace the success of others, as it helps them grow and pushes them to think differently. One principal with whom we spoke described how every time he went to one of his colleagues' schools, he came away with a new idea of how to improve some aspect of his school. This often related to improving the school's physical environment. He worked with one colleague who was always finding ways to enhance the physical appearance of the school with inspirational quotes on walls, student recognition boards, university banners displayed prominently, ceiling tiles featuring student artwork, and professional nameplates outside teachers' classrooms, including their photo and favorite quote. This principal said he always left the colleague's building feeling energized and committed to implementing the idea or improving upon it at his own school. He did not feel like less of a principal because the original idea was not his own.

Collaboration has a way of inspiring (or nudging) us to up our game. Competition means there must be a winner and a loser. This is not the case in collaboration. In collaboration, we can all win. We find the difference between competition and collaboration is simply in the eye of the beholder. If you think someone else having success means you are losing, then you view the world through the lens of competition. If someone else's success motivates you to be better or create a better environment for your students, you are a collaborator. Principled principals lead their teachers to collaborate for the benefit of teacher performance and student learning. They model this by collaborating with fellow principals for the benefit of the entire district and their own school.

Know When to Say, "When"

Collaboration is a key ingredient to the success of any school or organization. The time has long passed when we believed we could do great things all on our own. We know beyond a shadow of a doubt that working together in a productive and collaborative way will lead to greater outcomes. That said, it is important never to sacrifice your values for the sake of compromise. Compromise is very different from collaboration. One thing great principals never do is sacrifice their professional values for the sake of expedient compromise.

A retired superintendent we know used to tell the story that he attended every school board meeting with a letter of resignation in the pocket of his suit jacket. It wasn't that he wanted to quit his job or that he was anxious for the opportunity to resign. He had a good relationship with his school board, and they mostly saw eye to eye on all decisions. But as he explained it, he never knew when their views and decisions might veer from his moral and ethical values as a leader. He knew what his core values were, and should they no longer align with that of the school board, he was ready to submit his resignation with no hard feelings. We've thought about that story a lot. On the one hand, it might seem that having a resignation letter handy could lead to a rash decision he would later regret, but our most important takeaway is about the resolve of this leader. This superintendent is a person of great integrity who always had a "students first" focus. Being a principled principal means knowing when to say, "when," both for yourself and for your school.

We have known many principals who remain at schools long after they should have departed for a different role or school. We usually discover one of two reasons principals should seek new opportunities: The first is that the principal is unsuccessful in leading the current school. The second is that they have been quite successful, but it's simply time for a change so all parties can grow to new levels.

The first issue is probably the one we see most. Remember the question we posed in The Talent Principle chapter of this book: How long does it take to know you have made a poor hiring decision when it comes to classroom teachers? We believe the same can be asked about a principal. Within a couple of months into the school year, it is clear whether a principal is on the right track with staff, students, families, and the community. This isn't to say that the person is inherently a poor principal or cannot be supported to change course. That may be the case, but at the same time, it may simply be a poor fit, or the principal may never acquire the necessary leadership skills. Unfortunately, principals stay in positions where they are not leading the school to success much longer than they should. If a principal is not making at least some meaningful progress after an entire school year, it is time for the district to part ways with the principal and for the principal to recognize this too. As a principal, your foremost job is to successfully lead the school to support student learning. If the school you are leading is not in a better place after a year of your leadership, you should consider whether the school is still the right fit for you and whether you are the right leader for that school.

As a principal, your foremost job is to successfully lead the school to support student learning.

A second, albeit less common, situation is when a good principal stays too long. This is an odd thing to consider when many of us grew up in schools where the principal was a twenty-year veteran at the same school. When we were students ourselves, it seemed that the principalship was a job a person accepted once and then finished out their career in that role at a single school. While there still may be principals who serve one school for twenty or thirty years, we suspect this has become, and will remain, the exception rather than the norm.

When a good principal has taken a school as far as he or she can, it is time for fresh ideas and new leadership. Even good principals can overstay their tenure at a school. Sometimes new eyes on old problems are all it takes to jumpstart a school to another level. Great principals know when they have taken a school as far as they can, and they move on to help other schools. There is nothing inherently negative about leadership changes as long as they are the right changes at the right time.

A good example of this is with a principal we know in the Chicago area. She helped lead her school in implementing 1:1 learning, transforming the classroom learning environment for students and teachers. This principal helped teachers grow professionally, improved parent communication and involvement, and saw student academic achievement data rise significantly. After serving five years as principal, the school she led was in a great place. It was at this point in time that the principal was approached by another district inquiring about making the exact changes this principal had made and seeking guidance on making similar changes in their own district. Although it was a difficult decision, this principal ultimately decided to leave her school and take the position in the district that was just about to begin their own 1:1 learning implementation. Why would anyone do this?

When we talked to the principal, her answer was quite simple: She thought she could help the other school and make a bigger difference there than she could at her current school. Her feeling was that she had taken her current school to a great place, and now someone new could come in and build on the success to take it to another level—with a new set of skills that she did not possess. She also felt she had the specific knowledge to support her new school in its mission to create more engaging learning for its students. She felt she could help teachers, students, and parents in the transition just like she had done before. Her personal mission was to help as many students and teachers as possible, regardless of the school she served at the moment.

When she left, the school was operating as a true professional learning community. Much of the success she had enjoyed had to do with her penchant for organizing staff members into productive working teams focused on common goals. Almost every staff member held her in the highest regard, and many were devastated when they learned she was leaving. Yet the new school she would be leading was not known for a collaborative culture, and this principal believed her skills as an effective team member and team builder would benefit the new school more than her current one.

Where some saw it as a move from a high-performing school to a more challenging school and perhaps even a "step down," she saw it as a challenge and an opportunity. Principled principals seem to constantly exhort students and staff members to take risks. They are not afraid to take risks themselves—even when that means deciding to leave a fantastic professional situation for a new and challenging one.

The Collaboration Principle
3–2–1

3

PRINCIPALS' PERSPECTIVES ON THE COLLABORATION PRINCIPLE

Jessica Johnson (@PrincipalJ) is the elementary school principal and District Assessment Coordinator at Dodgeland School District in Juneau, Wisconsin. She was the 2014 Wisconsin National Distinguished Principal. She is also an adjunct professor for the Educational Leadership Department at Viterbo University and has coauthored *The Coach Approach to School Leadership: Leading Teachers to Higher Levels of Effectiveness* and *Breaking Out of Isolation: Becoming a Connected School Leader*. Jessica builds in time at her school to ensure collaboration can happen so students receive a guaranteed and viable curriculum in all classrooms across grade levels:

> Collaboration for the principled principal takes place in multiple avenues. It is essential for all educators in a school to collaborate to ensure that everyone is on the same page for students' success. As a building leader, I collaborate daily with many educators in my building in quick conversations, which may be to follow up on a student issue or check in with my secretary on the day's agenda. Many teachers do the same regarding where they are in teaching

a unit or how their students performed on a quick check. As the building leader, it is essential to intentionally schedule in time to support teams to collaborate with the purpose of ensuring alignment of curriculum and instruction.

I'll be honest; this can pose a challenge when teachers don't see eye to eye or just want to do it their own way, but this work is imperative to create a school-wide system that ensures all students get the education they deserve. This allows me to confidently tell parents it doesn't matter which teacher they get—our school does not have a lottery system.

When educators authentically collaborate on the work that matters, we build professional trust. When we don't have professional trust, it might look like this:

- The high school math teachers blame the middle school math teachers for never teaching students to solve a linear equation.
- The middle school English language arts teachers blame the elementary teachers for never teaching students to write an informative essay.
- The third-grade teacher just knows whenever she gets students from "Mr. Garrett," they will most likely be below level in reading.
- The elementary and middle school teachers get frustrated to hear what happens to their students as they move on to the next building level.

Does any of this sound familiar? These things happen when we don't have the professional trust to know we have solid alignments across all levels to ensure all students in our school/district are set up for success.

Being a principal can be lonely and isolating because there is no one in your building with a similar role with whom you can have conversations about the work you do every day. But it doesn't have to be this way. I continue to grow and learn each day from principals and educators across the country/world in my Professional

Learning Network (PLN). This starts on Twitter and moves to deeper conversations in Voxer, which I benefit from tremendously. I am grateful for the many educators who take their time to not only share ideas on Twitter or Voxer but to even collaborate by contributing resources into a shared Google doc from which we can all benefit. It is not the same kind of deep, collaborative work that happens in a school, but it is an amazing way to share the great things happening in schools despite our geographical distance.

Kelley McCall (@mccall_kelley) is principal at Graber Elementary School in Hutchinson, Kansas. Kelley was an elementary school teacher at St. Thomas Aquinas and Valley Center Public Schools for ten years before joining Graber. She is also the cofounder of *Moms As Principals*, a moderator for the *Principals in Action* chat, and a Code.org Affiliate. She also blogs for her website, *The Inspired Principal*. Kelley not only cultivates collaborative practices within the school she leads but also models the importance of collaboration in her own professional learning:

> If I were to pick one thing that makes me proud to be the principal of Graber Elementary School, it would have to be how well we collaborate to make sure our students are successful. While many of our students have experienced severe trauma and poverty, most of my team were blessed with a happy childhood. Because we don't always understand where our students are coming from, it's imperative that we work together to find solutions for those who are not considered "universal" students. Collaboration has become our go-to whenever we are looking for creative methods to solve a student concern and support the teachers who work with them.
>
> As the lead learner of the building, I make it my mission to bring in the right players to each student support meeting. It is important to me to have the classroom teachers, our special

education department, counselor, school psychologist, and social worker all in the room when we collaborate. I believe each of them brings an expertise to the table that allows us to look at the whole child. I do my best to offer suggestions, find resources, and possibly remove roadblocks that may stand in our way of success.

It is also important that I not just talk the talk. I must model the behaviors I wish to see among my staff. I encourage a growth mindset, am willing to take risks, and trust the experience my staff brings to the table. I encourage and respect different points of view. I will even push them to try new things that might not feel comfortable at first, but I am always willing to work alongside them to put it into place.

Modeling how to build a professional learning network outside of our building's four walls is also beneficial. I turn to the Principals in Action and Moms As Principals PLNs to grow as a leader. During my daily commute, I connect, collaborate, and learn with principals from all over the country. If I have a question or concern, my PLN is always willing to provide ideas and guidance. They encourage me when I'm down and celebrate my successes. Without my PLN, this job would be lonely and probably lead to burnout; instead, I'm a better leader and excited to go to work every day.

Leah Whitford (@leah_whit) is principal at Winskill Elementary School in the Lancaster, Wisconsin, School Community district. Leah is always on the lookout for opportunities to collaborate with other educators in an effort to improve as a leader. She is active on Twitter and enjoys attending Edcamps and other professional learning events. In her school, she not only focuses on staff members collaborating effectively, but also collaborates intentionally with parents and students to ensure their perspectives are heard—and this has helped Winskill School become much better:

When we think of collaboration as school administrators, it is usually in connection with other administrators or with teachers. Those are definitely important collaborative partnerships, to be sure, but there are others to be considered as well.

The partnership between the instructional leader and parents is also a vital one. Parents bring a voice to the conversation that has often been ignored or turned to mute. I have found that by inviting parents to the table, we have been able to address issues that would have otherwise gone unresolved or would have been aired on social media, where nothing resolved well. We've been able to make changes, often very simple ones, which have had a huge impact on the lives of the children entrusted to our care. Having this other perspective has been critical to the work we've done to strengthen our connections to the community.

I've also found that collaborating with students can have a powerful impact on our school. Late last fall, a group of girls asked to meet with me about our morning announcements. You just have to love kids' honesty:

"Sorry, Mrs. W, but they are kinda boring."

Having heard me say, "It's not enough to come forward with a problem; you need to come forward with solutions too," they came prepared. They asked if they could take over the morning announcements. They had written a sample script, had a list of songs with which to start the day, and ideas for other additions to the announcements. Over the course of several lunch hour meetings along with the use of Google docs, these girls and I worked together to fine-tune their script, making sure they were including all the key points and double-checking the lyrics of their songs to ensure that only "school appropriate" songs were being played. As a side note, one of the most exciting pieces of this collaborative effort was that one of the girls was an English Language Learner (ELL) student who had virtually no English speaking fluency when she joined us the previous spring; however, because of the support of her peers, who helped her practice and made sure her scripted lines were appropriate for her English accessibility, she felt confident enough to not only help write the announcements but serve as a morning announcer. That was incredibly powerful for those of us who knew her! Because these girls were all moving on to the middle school at the end of the year, they recognized that they would need someone to take over their work. Working together, they trained a new team of "Arrow Announcers." Interestingly, some of the boys in the upcoming fifth-grade class spoke up about the need to make this group a boy/girl combination and volunteered to be part of the announcement team.

Every day I am able to experience firsthand the impact collaboration can have when the adults in the school, local, and global community learn and work together towards meeting common goals. Most exciting for me is the impact collaboration can have on the future of our students when they are encouraged and empowered to work together to solve problems.

2

HARMONY PRINCIPLE RESOURCES

For a list of these and other resources,
please visit theprincipledprincipal.com.

"Ladder of Collaboration"

This handout from Great Results Team Building illustrates the progression and evolution of positive teamwork behaviors, with the rungs of the ladder ranging from "Confusion" at the lowest level to "Collaboration" at the top rung. The two ends of the ladder, "Consideration" and "Communication" are equally important, as we will never reach the top rung without concern for, and knowledge of, others in our schools.

"The New Power of Collaboration"

In this TED Talk, Howard Rheingold, a critic, writer, and teacher who focuses on the cultural, social, and political implications of modern communication media and virtual communities, talks about the world of collaboration, participatory media, and collective action—and how Wikipedia is really an outgrowth of our natural human instinct to work as a group.

1

COLLABORATION PRINCIPLE CULTURE CRUSHER

In the introduction of this book, we shared a list of "culture crushers" brainstormed by a group of principals with whom we worked in one district. The list includes the following four behaviors:

1. When competition supersedes collaboration
2. Teachers who act as bullies to other teachers
3. Teachers who cannot celebrate their colleague's successes
4. Jealousy and cliques among colleagues

When these behaviors exist in a school, we are destroying the culture of that school. These behaviors are all related to the Collaboration Principle; moreover, they also apply at the district level, not just the school level. We have seen the same behaviors—and their opposite behaviors—in large school districts' leadership teams.

In schools and districts in which true collaboration exists, educators value teamwork over competing to see who can be "best." They know that in schools where adults display "bullying" behaviors, kids are more likely to do so as well, so they never bully a colleague. They celebrate the successes of their colleagues without wondering if and when they will be recognized. They work to eradicate jealousy and cliques among students and start by avoiding such behaviors and groups themselves.

Principled principals build the culture by promoting authentic collaboration in every team setting in which they take part. They know collaboration creates connections and networks that can help the team, as well as each individual on the team, get better for the benefit of the students they serve.

CONCLUSION
Principals Leading with Principles

We need to learn to set our course by the stars, not by the lights of every passing ship.
—Gen. Omar Bradley

When we started exploring the idea for this book, our goal was to identify and describe the principles that inform the leadership of great school principals. Our hope is that these ten principles, the examples, the resources, and the knowledge shared by thirty of the finest principals from around the country not only provide helpful guidance for school leaders but also validation for all the good work so many principals are already doing. We are convinced that successful principals lead with principles. These principles guide their actions, their words, their decisions, and their professional judgment.

As we began writing this book and considering the ten principles we deemed most representative of those guiding great principals, we came to the early realization that each of these ten principles helped build, support, and maintain one thing: a positive, productive school culture.

As we noted at the very beginning of this book, school principals *do* impact student learning in the school; however, the principal is not the one designing and delivering daily learning experiences for students, which is why teachers are still the greatest influencers of a child's learning. The principal's impact on student learning is more distal than that of the teacher. The principal does, however, make the most impact on a school in the form of that school's culture.

> ## Great principals understand it is their number one job to build and support a positive school culture of high expectations for all: every student, every staff member, and every family.

School culture can impact the ABCs (attitudes, behaviors, and commitments) of the teachers, students, and families who comprise the school community. All ten principles described in this book impact a school's culture. From whom we hire, and why, to how we communicate, and when, each aspect of each principle becomes embedded into the school's culture when done consistently over time. Our belief is that principals who lead with these ten principles are impacting their school culture in substantial and positive ways. Great principals understand it is their number one job to build and support a positive school culture of high expectations for all: every student, every staff member, and every family.

Do You Trust Me?

Another early realization at which we arrived as we began this book was the fact that trust played a role in so many of the principles; in fact, when searching the final document, we discovered we used the word "trust" forty-five times throughout the book. One of the indispensable traits any leader needs to exhibit, without fail, and expect from others is trust.

In schools with a positive culture, teachers believe the leader cares about them and has their best interests in mind. The principal, in turn, trusts that teachers want what's best for the school and each student attending the school. Leading with principles will not only support your culture, but it will also build trust in your relationships with staff, students, and families.

One of the key behaviors to develop trust among those we lead is doing what we say we will do. When you lead with principles such as the ones outlined in this book, you are clearly outlining for everyone what your values are and what you stand for. Leading with principles allows people to understand and come to terms with the values of the leader. Over time, people at the school can anticipate what is going to happen in terms of solutions and responses when common problems arise.

As you likely have noticed by now, we love quotes of all kinds and began this book with one of our favorites: "When you base your life on principles, most of your decisions are already made before you encounter them." This truth should provide comfort to leaders that their principles can and will inform their decisions. This also means when those we lead know what our principles are, they can better understand the decisions that are made and the direction in which the organization is heading. When everyone in the school community knows what is happening and, more importantly, *why* it is happening, it helps them feel safe and in control.

In the vitally important relationship between a principal and a teacher, this is called *trust.* In a school where teachers do not trust the principal or the principal does not trust teachers, culture is toxic and a counterproductive force on the growth of its students. The single most important word in any relationship is *trust,* and principled principals work to establish trust among all school community members—starting with themselves. Successful principals are trustworthy people.

Substance versus Style

A third realization we had while writing this book had to do with the "substance" of great principals combined with the "styles" of great principals. Great principals need to have a combination of substance and style. Although we have known many successful principals whose "style" is a bit understated (i.e., they were quiet by nature, not very flashy, even introverted), we do not know any successful principals who are not men and women of substance, meaning people who know their stuff and take the time to learn about education, about leadership, about their schools, about their teachers, and about their students.

We have found that the best leaders never compromise substance for style. A good example is the idea of branding your school. Many teachers, principals, schools, and districts have taken to telling their school's story through a variety of social media platforms. They use Twitter, YouTube, Facebook, Instagram, and other platforms to connect with parents, other educators, and the world to tell their school's true story. This is a wonderful example of twenty-first-century progress in our schools, and we fully support the idea of teachers, principals, and schools sharing all the good things happening in their classrooms. The way in which we now tell these stories is an example of style. The messages we are sending may be about "style" too: how engaged our students are, how much they love school, how much the teachers love them, and so on. Yet underneath whatever tools we use to tell our school's story, or the fun stories we are telling, there needs to be substance, or the style eventually rings hollow.

It is not enough to Tweet to your school's hashtag a picture of students with the message *"Students having fun in math today!"* There must be substance behind that in the form of actual learning. Saying it or Tweeting it does not automatically make it true. We need to move beyond telling our school's story to showing our school's story, including showing how kids and staff members are growing and applying what they're learning to move from *meaning seekers* to *meaning makers.*

We need to move beyond telling our school's story to *showing* our school's story.

We worked with one principal who embodied a perfect blend of substance and style. He was known for wearing red hi-top Converse sneakers along with his suit and tie every day. He learned how to do magic tricks so he could perform for students at his school on special occasions. He served at a large campus, so he was known for riding a scooter throughout the hallways of the school and visiting classrooms regularly. He was known to occasionally sing on the morning announcements. During the holidays, he dressed up as a train conductor and read aloud *The Polar Express* at a faculty meeting as the sole agenda item. He was energetic, charismatic, always "on," and forever thinking of new ways to make teaching and learning fun.

If you asked students and staff at the school about him, you would almost certainly hear about some of his zany antics that contributed to his leadership style. Yet, if you dug a bit deeper, you would also hear that this principal was serious when it came to student learning and teacher performance. He had extremely high expectations for himself as a leader and equally high expectations for every teacher and student at the school. He was a former science teacher, but made it his mission to learn the English language arts and math standards inside out. He knew the names of every student at this large school and knew where they stood academically. When the new Common Core State Standards were released, he was the first person in his district to learn them and took the primary role in training his staff about these new standards, knowing they would impact everyone at the school. This principal truly knew his stuff. Because of his style, nearly every student and staff member genuinely liked this principal as a person. Because of his substance, he was also the most respected principal in the entire area.

The principles we live by in our schools help to make our stories more substantive, more real. It is not enough to say we *believe* all kids can learn; we must make that statement a reality on a daily basis through our actions and interactions.

Principles are the foundation for the good stories we want to tell about our schools and about public education. Leading with principles is all about making sure our school's culture has the substance to back up the style. All great principals have a certain style, and we believe this is an important part of what makes them successful. Their style as the leader of the school impacts the culture and often adds the "fun factor" to the hard work everyone in the school puts in each day. These same principals, however, never subordinate, in importance, substance for style.

Standing on Principle

Being a leader takes courage. It is certainly easy to bask in the limelight when things are going well. It is quite another thing to feel the chill when a plan didn't work out the way we intended or an initiative fails to take root, and we have to start all over.

Leading is not for the faint of heart, which is why we love leaders. We have the utmost respect for leaders at any level who put themselves on the line so the group can move forward. We believe people are called to lead, not for money or notoriety, but because they believe they can make a positive difference in the lives of others. So when the skies do become dark, and the storm approaches, it is important to remember we are never alone if we stand on principles. Our foundation is always there and, with it, is the comfort of knowing what we are doing is right for students, staff, and parents.

> ## It is important to remember we are never alone if we stand on principles.

We believe the ten principles outlined in this book are important to the success of school leaders. Great principals live these principles, day in and day out—during good times and bad. It is important to note, however, that these same principals are neither rigid nor authoritarian leaders. Although it is true they live and lead with non-negotiable principles, they are masters of adapting to change. And their willingness to change and lead others through times of change is one of the ten principles of effective principals. Somewhat paradoxically, though, there is something within these leaders that never changes, which actually contributes to their ability to embrace change and lead change. The part of them that never changes—their core principles—allows them to lead change effectively. This is a leadership behavior essential in today's schools—places that are increasingly epicenters of change.

The life of a school principal is beyond demanding. We have held no other job as difficult and draining. It is also one of the most important jobs we can imagine. We salute school leaders for taking on this challenging yet rewarding work.

Thank you for standing on principles in your service as school leaders. You are making a difference.

REFERENCES

Introduction

Couros, George. *The Innovator's Mindset: Empower Learning, Unleash Talent, and Lead a Culture of Creativity.* San Diego, California: Dave Burgess Consulting, Inc., 2015.

Leithwood, Kenneth, Karen Seashore Louis, Stephen Anderson, and Kyla Wahlstrom. *How Leadership Influences Student Learning.* Ontario: The Wallace Foundation, 2004.

Marzano, Robert J., Timothy Waters and Brian A. Mcnulty, *School Leadership That Works: From Research to Results.* Alexandria, Virginia: ASCD, 2005.

Principle 1

Partnership for Assessment of Readiness for College and Careers, parcc-assessment.org/released-items.

Durlak, Joseph A., Celene E. Domitrovich, Roger P. Weissberg, and Thomas P. Gullotta. *Handbook of Social and Emotional Learning: Research and Practice.* New York, New York: Guilford Press, 2017.

"Double Jeopardy: How Third Grade Reading Skills and Poverty Influence High School Graduation," *The Annie E. Casey Foundation,* aecf.org/resources/double-jeopardy.

Nguyen Barry, Mary, and Michael Dannenberg, "Out of Pocket: The High Cost of Inadequate High Schools and High School Student Achievement on College Affordability," *Education Reform Now*, April 2016, edreformnow.org/policy-briefs/out-of-pocket-the-high-cost-of-inadequate-high-schools-and-high-school-student-achievement-on-college-affordability.

Couros, George. *The Innovator's Mindset: Empower Learning, Unleash Talent, and Lead a Culture of Creativity.* San Diego, California: Dave Burgess Consulting, Inc., 2015.

Principle 2
Goodwin, Doris Kearns. *Team of Rivals: The Political Genius of Abraham Lincoln.* New York, New York: Simon & Schuster Paperbacks, 2006.

Zoul, Jeffrey, and Todd Whitaker. *4 CORE Factors for School Success.* New York, New York: Routledge, 2008.

Principle 3
McConnell, Anthony. "The Perceived Self-Leadership Capacity of K–5 Principals in Illinois and its Correlation to Student Achievement." Doctoral Dissertation, 2017.

Principle 4
Collins, Jim. *Good to Great: Why Some Companies Make the Leap and Others Don't.* New York, New York: HarperCollins, 2001.

Merriam-Webster, s.v., "Outcome," merriam-webster.com/dictionary/outcome.

Principle 5
Bryant, Adam. "In Head-Hunting, Big Data May Not Be Such a Big Deal." *New York Times* (New York, NY), June 19, 2013.

Lencioni, Patrick. *The Advantage: Why Organizational Health Trumps Everything Else in Business.* San Francisco, California: Jossey-Bass, 2012.

Principle 6
Kotter, John P. *A Sense of Urgency.* Boston, Massachusetts: Harvard Business School Publishing, 2008.

Coles, Paul, et all, "The Toxic Terabyte." *IBM Global Technology Services*. July 2006. ibm.com/services/no/cio/leverage/levinfo_wp_gts_thetoxic.pdf.

Bridges, William, and Susan Bridges. *Managing Transitions: Making the Most of Change*. Philadelphia, Pennsylvania: Da Capo Press, 2009.

Principle 7
"What Is Bullying?" *stopbullying.gov,* stopbullying.gov/what-is-bullying/index.html.

Sinanis, Tony, and Joseph M. Sanfelippo. *The Power of Branding: Telling Your School's Story*. Thousand Oaks, California: Corwin, 2015.

Smith, Aaron. "Record shares of Americans now own smartphones, have home broadband." *Pew Research Center*, January 12, 2017, pewresearch.org/fact-tank/2017/01/12/evolution-of-technology/.

Principle 9
Adams, Susan. "The Happiest and Unhappiest Jobs in 2015." *Forbes.com*, February 26, 2015, forbes.com/sites/susanadams/2015/02/26/the-happiest-and-unhappiest-jobs-in-2015.

ACKNOWLEDGMENTS

Writing any book is always a rewarding, yet challenging, undertaking. Although only two names appear as authors on the cover of this book, this work—like all our other writing projects—has been a collaborative effort and could not have been accomplished without the wisdom, support, and contributions of many individuals, far too many to thank individually by name in this space. We would be remiss, however, if we did not publicly acknowledge our appreciation to the following people, without whom this book never would have been published:

First, we are indebted to the thirty principals who graciously added their voices to this book. These distinguished school leaders are among the finest we know in our entire profession, and we are humbled that they were all willing to drop what they were doing to contribute their own reflections on school leadership in order to assist us and make this a more practical resource for others. Thank you for serving as genuine role models for all of us who are passionate about leadership!

In addition, we wish to acknowledge the support and encouragement of Dave and Shelley Burgess. Thank you for believing in us!

We also wish to acknowledge the excellence of educators in the Deerfield Public Schools District 109 in Deerfield, Illinois. We have been honored to serve on the Deerfield team, and several of the stories, insights, and resources in this book emanate from our time working in this wonderful community. Thank you for your willingness to take risks and lead the way!

Finally, we want to acknowledge and thank Brad Black, Jared Northup, and the team at HUMANeX Ventures for creating the custom culture and talent survey resources included in this book.

Bring Jeff Zoul or Anthony McConnell to Your School or Event

Jeff and Anthony provide engaging, high-energy, and practical keynote presentations, workshops, and professional learning opportunities. They provide these services both individually and together when requested. Having served in a variety of roles in education, Jeff and Anthony rely on their insights gleaned from their vast experiences to inspire and equip educators to continuously improve their skills as teachers, learners, and leaders.

To receive additional information about bringing Jeff and/or Anthony to your school event, please connect with them via the following:

Jeff Zoul
Email: jeffzoul@gmail.com
Twitter @jeff_zoul

Anthony McConnell
Email: Mcconaw@gmail.com
Twitter: @mcconnellaw

More from
 Dave Burgess
Consulting, Inc.

Teach Like a PIRATE
Increase Student Engagement, Boost Your Creativity, and Transform Your Life as an Educator
By Dave Burgess (@BurgessDave)

Teach Like a PIRATE is the *New York Times* best-selling book that has sparked a worldwide educational revolution. It is part inspirational manifesto that ignites passion for the profession and part practical road map, filled with dynamic strategies to dramatically increase student engagement. Translated into multiple languages, its message resonates with educators who want to design outrageously creative lessons and transform school into a life-changing experience for students.

Learn Like a PIRATE
Empower Your Students to Collaborate, Lead, and Succeed
By Paul Solarz (@PaulSolarz)

Today's job market demands that students be prepared to take responsibility for their lives and careers. We do them a disservice if we teach them how to earn passing grades without equipping them to take charge of their education. Learn how to design classroom experiences that encourage students to take risks and explore their passions in a stimulating, motivating, and supportive environment where improvement, rather than grades, is the focus. Discover how student-led classrooms help students thrive and develop into self-directed, confident citizens who are capable of making smart, responsible decisions, all on their own.

P is for PIRATE
Inspirational ABCs for Educators
By Dave and Shelley Burgess
(@Burgess_Shelley)

Teaching is an adventure that stretches the imagination and calls for creativity every day! In *P is for PIRATE*, husband and wife team Dave and Shelley Burgess encourage and inspire educators to make their classrooms fun and exciting places to learn. Tapping into years of personal experience and drawing on the insights of more than seventy educators, the authors offer a wealth of ideas for making learning and teaching more fulfilling than ever before.

Play Like a Pirate
Engage Students with Toys, Games, and Comics
By Quinn Rollins (@jedikermit)

Yes! School can be simultaneously fun and educational. In *Play Like a Pirate*, Quinn Rollins offers practical, engaging strategies and resources that make it easy to integrate fun into your curriculum. Regardless of the grade level you teach, you'll find inspiration and ideas that will help you engage your students in unforgettable ways.

eXPlore Like a Pirate
Gamification and Game-Inspired Course Design to Engage, Enrich, and Elevate Your Learners
By Michael Matera (@MrMatera)

Are you ready to transform your classroom into an experiential world that flourishes on collaboration and creativity? Then set sail with classroom game designer and educator Michael Matera as he reveals the possibilities and power of game-based learning. Learn how to apply gamification strategies that will work with and enhance (rather than replace) your current curriculum and discover how these engaging methods can be applied to any grade level or subject.

The Innovator's Mindset
Empower Learning, Unleash Talent,
and Lead a Culture of Creativity
By George Couros (@gcouros)

The traditional system of education requires students to hold their questions and compliantly stick to the scheduled curriculum. But our job as educators is to provide new and better opportunities for our students. It's time to recognize that compliance doesn't foster innovation, encourage critical thinking, or inspire creativity—and those are the skills our students need to succeed. George Couros encourages teachers and administrators to empower their learners to wonder, to explore—and to become forward-thinking leaders.

Master the Media
How Teaching Media Literacy Can
Save Our Plugged-in World
By Julie Smith (@julnilsmith)

Written to help teachers and parents educate the next generation, *Master the Media* explains the history, purpose, and messages behind the media. The point isn't to get kids to unplug; it's to help them make informed choices, understand the difference between truth and lies, and discern perception from reality. Critical thinking leads to smarter decisions—and it's why media literacy can save the world.

The Zen Teacher
Creating FOCUS, SIMPLICITY, and
TRANQUILITY in the Classroom
By Dan Tricarico (@TheZenTeacher)

Teachers have incredible power to influence—even improve—the future. Educator, blogger, and speaker Dan Tricarico provides practical, easy-to-use techniques to help teachers be their best so they can maximize their performance and improve their quality of life. Learn what it means to develop a Zen practice—something that has nothing to do with religion and everything to do with your ability to thrive in the classroom.

Lead Like a PIRATE
Make School Amazing for Your Students and Staff
By Shelley Burgess and Beth Houf
(@Burgess_Shelley, @BethHouf)

Education leaders Shelley Burgess and Beth Houf map out the character traits necessary to captain a school or district. You'll learn where to find the treasure that's already in your classrooms and schools—and how to bring out the very best in your educators. This book will equip and encourage you to be relentless in your quest to make school amazing for your students, staff, parents, and communities.

50 Things You Can Do with Google Classroom
By Alice Keeler and Libbi Miller
(@AliceKeeler, @MillerLibbi)

It can be challenging to add new technology to the classroom, but it's a must if students are going to be well-equipped for the future. Alice Keeler and Libbi Miller shorten the learning curve by providing a thorough overview of the Google Classroom App. Complete with screenshots, *50 Things You Can Do with Google Classroom* provides ideas and step-by-step instructions to help teachers implement this powerful tool.

50 Things to Go Further with Google Classroom
A Student-Centered Approach
By Alice Keeler and Libbi Miller
(@AliceKeeler, @MillerLibbi)

Today's technology empowers educators to move away from the traditional classroom where teachers lead and students work independently—each doing the same thing. Authors and educators Alice Keeler and Libbi Miller offer inspiration and resources to help you create a digitally rich, engaging, student-centered environment. They show you how to tap into the power of individualized learning that is possible with Google Classroom.

Pure Genius
*Building a Culture of Innovation and
Taking 20% Time to the Next Level*
By Don Wettrick (@DonWettrick)

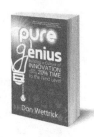

For far too long, schools have been bastions of boredom, killers of creativity, and way too comfortable with compliance and conformity. In *Pure Genius*, Don Wettrick explains how collaboration—with experts, students, and other educators—can help you create interesting, and even life-changing, opportunities for learning. Wettrick's book inspires and equips educators with a systematic blueprint for teaching innovation in any school.

140 Twitter Tips for Educators
*Get Connected, Grow Your Professional
Learning Network, and Reinvigorate Your Career*
By Brad Currie, Billy Krakower, and Scott Rocco
(@bradmcurrie, @wkrakower, @ScottRRocco)

Whatever questions you have about education or about how you can be even better at your job, you'll find ideas, resources, and a vibrant network of professionals ready to help you on Twitter. #Satchat hosts and founders of Evolving Educators, Brad Currie, Billy Krakower, and Scott Rocco, offer step-by-step instructions to help you master the basics of Twitter, build an online following, and become a Twitter rock star.

Ditch That Textbook
*Free Your Teaching and Revolutionize
Your Classroom*
By Matt Miller (@jmattmiller)

Textbooks are symbols of centuries-old education. They're often outdated as soon as they hit students' desks. It's time to ditch those textbooks—and those textbook assumptions about learning! Teacher and blogger Matt Miller provides a support system, toolbox, and manifesto to help educators free their teaching and revolutionize their classrooms.

How Much Water Do We Have?
5 Success Principles for Conquering Any Challenge and Thriving in Times of Change
By Pete Nunweiler with Kris Nunweiler

Pete Nunweiler identifies five key elements—information, planning, motivation, support, and leadership—that are necessary for the success of any goal, life transition, or challenge. If you're feeling stressed out or uncertain at work or at home, this book will show you how to find, acquire, and use the these key elements so you can share them with your team and family members.

Instant Relevance
Using Today's Experiences to Teach Tomorrow's Lessons
By Denis Sheeran (@MathDenisNJ)

Every day, students in schools around the world ask the question, "When am I ever going to use this in real life?" In *Instant Relevance*, author and keynote speaker Denis Sheeran equips you to create engaging lessons *from* experiences and events that matter to your students. Learn how to help your students see meaningful connections between the real world and what they learn in the classroom—because that's when learning sticks.

The Classroom Chef
Sharpen Your Lessons. Season Your Classes. Make Math Meaningful.
By John Stevens and Matt Vaudrey
(@Jstevens009, @MrVaudrey)

In *The Classroom Chef*, math teachers and instructional coaches John Stevens and Matt Vaudrey share their secret recipes, ingredients, and tips for serving up lessons that engage students and help them "get" math. You can use these ideas and methods as-is, or better yet, tweak them and create your own enticing educational meals. The message the authors share is that, with imagination and preparation, every teacher can be a classroom chef.

Start. Right. Now.

Teach and Lead for Excellence

By Todd Whitaker, Jeff Zoul, and Jimmy Casas
(@ToddWhitaker, @Jeff_Zoul, @casas_jimmy)

In their work leading up to *Start. Right. Now.*, Todd Whitaker, Jeff Zoul, and Jimmy Casas studied educators from across the nation and discovered four key behaviors of excellence: Excellent leaders and teachers *Know the Way, Show the Way, Go the Way,* and *Grow Each Day.* If you are ready to take the first step toward excellence, this motivating book will put you on the right path.

The Writing on the Classroom Wall

How Posting Your Most Passionate Beliefs about Education Can Empower Your Students, Propel Your Growth, and Lead to a Lifetime of Learning

By Steve Wyborney (@SteveWyborney)

Steve Wyborney explains how posting and discussing Big Ideas can lead to deeper learning. You'll learn why sharing your ideas will sharpen and refine them. You'll also be encouraged to know that the Big Ideas you share don't have to be profound to make a profound impact on learning. In fact, it's okay if some of your ideas fall *off* the wall. What matters most is sharing them.

LAUNCH

Using Design Thinking to Boost Creativity and Bring Out the Maker in Every Student

By John Spencer and A.J. Juliani
(@spencerideas, @ajjuliani)

Something happens in students when they define themselves as *makers* and *inventors* and *creators.* They discover powerful skills—problem-solving, critical thinking, and imagination—that will help them shape the world's future. John Spencer and A.J. Juliani provide a process that can be incorporated into every class at every grade level, even if you don't consider yourself a "creative teacher."

241

Kids Deserve It!
Pushing Boundaries and Challenging Conventional Thinking
By Todd Nesloney and Adam Welcome
(@TechNinjaTodd, @awelcome)

In *Kids Deserve It!*, Todd and Adam encourage you to think big and make learning fun and meaningful for students. Their high-tech, high-touch, and highly engaging practices will inspire you to take risks, shake up the status quo, and be a champion for your students. While you're at it, you just might rediscover why you became an educator in the first place.

Escaping the School Leader's Dunk Tank
How to Prevail When Others Want to See You Drown
By Rebecca Coda and Rick Jetter
(@RebeccaCoda, @RickJetter)

No school leader is immune to the effects of discrimination, bad politics, revenge, or ego-driven coworkers. These kinds of dunk-tank situations can make an educator's life miserable. By sharing real-life stories and insightful research, the authors (who are dunk-tank survivors themselves) equip school leaders with the practical knowledge and emotional tools necessary to survive and, better yet, avoid getting "dunked."

Teaching Math with Google Apps
50 G Suite Activities
By Alice Keeler and Diana Herrington
(@AliceKeeler, @mathdiana)

Google Apps give teachers the opportunity to interact with students in a more meaningful way than ever before, while G Suite empowers students to be creative, critical thinkers who collaborate as they explore and learn. In *Teaching Math with Google Apps*, educators Alice Keeler and Diana Herrington demonstrate fifty different ways to bring math classes to the twenty-first century with easy-to-use technology.

Your School Rocks ... So Tell People!
*Passionately Pitch and Promote the
Positives Happening on Your Campus*
By Ryan McLane and Eric Lowe
(@McLane_Ryan, @EricLowe21)

Great things are happening in your school every day. The problem is, no one beyond your school walls knows about them. School principals Ryan McLane and Eric Lowe offer more than seventy immediately actionable tips along with easy-to-follow instructions and links to video tutorials. This practical guide equips you to create an effective and manageable communication strategy that will keep your students' families and community connected, informed, and excited about what's going on in your school.

Table Talk Math
*A Practical Guide for Bringing Math
into Everyday Conversations*
By John Stevens (@Jstevens009)

Making math part of families' everyday conversations is a powerful way to help children and teens learn to love math. In *Table Talk Math*, John Stevens offers parents (and teachers!) ideas for initiating authentic, math-based conversations that will get kids to notice and be curious about all the numbers, patterns, and equations in the world around them.

Shattering the Perfect Teacher Myth
*6 Truths That Will Help You THRIVE as an
Educator*
By Aaron Hogan (@aaron_hogan)

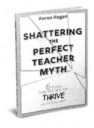

The idyllic myth of the perfect teacher perpetuates unrealistic expectations that erode self-confidence and set teachers up for failure. Author and educator Aaron Hogan is on a mission to shatter the myth of the perfect teacher by equipping educators with strategies that help them shift out of survival mode and THRIVE.

Shift This!
How to Implement Gradual Changes for
MASSIVE Impact in Your Classroom
By Joy Kirr (@JoyKirr)

Establishing a student-led culture that isn't focused on grades and homework but on individual responsibility and personalized learning may seem like a daunting task—especially if you think you have to do it all at once. But significant change is possible, sustainable, and even easy when it happens little by little. Learn how to make gradual shifts—in your thinking, teaching, and approach to classroom design—that will have a massive impact in your classroom. Make the first shift today!

Unmapped Potential
An Educator's Guide to Lasting Change
By Julie Hasson and Missy Lennard
(@PPrincipals)

No matter where you are in your educational career, chances are you have, at times, felt overwhelmed and overworked. Maybe you feel that way right now. If so, you aren't alone. But things can get better! You simply need the right map to guide you from frustrated to fulfilled. *Unmapped Potential* offers advice and practical strategies to help you find your unique path to becoming the kind of educator—the kind of person—you want to be.

Social LEADia
Moving Students from Digital Citizenship
to Digital Leadership
By Jennifer Casa-Todd (@JCasaTodd)

Equipping students for their futures begins by helping them become digital leaders now. In our networked society, students need to learn how to leverage social media to connect to people, passions, and opportunities to grow and make a difference. *Social LEADia* addresses the need to shift the conversations at school and at home from digital citizenship to digital leadership.

Spark Learning
3 Keys to Embracing the Power of Student Curiosity
By Ramsey Musallam (@ramusallam)

Inspired by his popular TED Talk "3 Rules to Spark Learning," this book combines brain science research, proven teaching methods, and Ramsey's personal story to empower you to improve your students' learning experiences by inspiring inquiry and harnessing its benefits. If you want to engage students in more interesting and effective learning, this is the book for you.

Ditch That Homework
Practical Strategies to Help Make Homework Obsolete
By Matt Miller and Alice Keeler
(@jmattmiller, @alicekeeler)

In *Ditch That Homework*, Matt Miller and Alice Keeler discuss the pros and cons of homework, why teachers assign it, and what life could look like without it. As they evaluate the research and share parent and teacher insights, the authors offer a convincing case for ditching homework and replacing it with more effective and personalized learning methods.

The Four O'Clock Faculty
A Rogue Guide to Revolutionizing Professional Development
By Rich Czyz (@RACzyz)

Author Rich Czyz is on a mission to revolutionize professional learning for all educators. In *The Four O'Clock Faculty*, Rich identifies ways to make professional development (PD) meaningful, efficient, and, above all, personally relevant. This book is a practical guide that reveals why some PD is so awful and what you can do to change the model for the betterment of you and your colleagues.

Culturize

Every Student. Every Day. Whatever It Takes.
By Jimmy Casas (@casas_jimmy)

In *Culturize*, author and education leader Jimmy Casas shares insights into what it takes to cultivate a community of learners who embody the innately human traits our world desperately needs, such as kindness, honesty, and compassion. His stories reveal how these "soft skills" can be honed while meeting and exceeding academic standards of twenty-first-century learning.

Code Breaker

Increase Creativity, Remix Assessment, and Develop a Class of Coder Ninjas!
By Brian Aspinall (@mraspinall)

Code Breaker equips you to use coding in your classroom to turn curriculum expectations into skills. Students learn how to identify problems, develop solutions, and use computational thinking to apply and demonstrate their learning. Best of all, you don't have to be a "computer geek" to empower your students with these essential skills.

The Wild Card

7 Steps to an Educator's Creative Breakthrough
By Hope and Wade King
(@hopekingteach, @wadeking7)

Have you ever wished you were more creative or that your students were more engaged in your lessons? The Wild Card is your step-by-step guide to experiencing a creative breakthrough in your classroom with your students. Hope and Wade King show you how to draw on your authentic self to deliver your content creatively and be the wild card who changes the game for your learners.

Stories from Webb

The Ideas, Passions, and Convictions of a Principal and His School Family

By Todd Nesloney (@TechNinjaTodd)

Stories from Webb goes right to the heart of education. Told by award-winning principal Todd Nesloney and his dedicated team of staff and teachers at Webb Elementary, this book will remind you why you became an educator. You'll be reinvigorated by these relatable stories—and you just may be inspired to tell your own!

About the Authors

 **Dr. Jeffrey Zoul** is a lifelong teacher, learner, and leader. During Jeff's distinguished career in education, he has served in a variety of roles, most recently as Assistant Superintendent for Teaching and Learning with Deerfield Public Schools District 109 in Deerfield, Illinois. Jeff also served as a teacher and coach in the State of Georgia for many years before moving into school administration.

Zoul has also taught graduate courses at the university level in the areas of assessment, research, and program evaluation. He is the author and coauthor of many books, including *What Connected Educators Do Differently, Start. Right. Now., Improving Your School One Week at a Time,* and *Leading Professional Learning.*

Jeff has earned several degrees, including his undergraduate degree from the University of Massachusetts and his doctoral degree from the University of Alabama. He has also been recognized for his work as an educational leader on numerous occasions. In his spare time, Jeff enjoys running and has completed over a dozen marathons. Zoul resides in Evanston, Illinois.

Jeff blogs at jeffreyzoul.blogspot.com. Please connect with him via Twitter at @jeff_zoul.

Anthony McConnell is the Assistant Superintendent for Teaching, Learning, and Innovation at Deerfield Public Schools District 109 in Deerfield, IL. Anthony began his career as a high school social studies and English language teacher at Rock Island High School in Rock Island, Illinois.

As a school administrator, Anthony has served as both an assistant principal and principal. As principal of Kipling Elementary School in Deerfield, Illinois, Anthony led the school in construction of STEM learning spaces, implementation of 1:1 learning, and adoption of The Leader in Me process.

In his final year as principal, Kipling was recognized as a National Blue Ribbon School of Excellence. Anthony obtained his bachelor's degree in history and anthropology from Western Kentucky University, a master's degree in English language learning from Western Governors University, and his master's degree and doctorate in educational leadership from Western Illinois University. Anthony also serves as an adjunct professor in educational leadership at Concordia University in River Forest, Illinois. In his spare time, he enjoys running, exercising, and spending time with his family: AJ, Aurelia, and Cayce. Anthony resides in Lake Villa, Illinois.

Anthony blogs at anthonymcconnell.edublogs.org. Please connect with him via Twitter at @mcconnellaw.

CPSIA information can be obtained
at www.ICGtesting.com
Printed in the USA
FSHW01n2135210918
52202FS